Presented to:

_____

From:

_____

# OASIS

## FOR MY

# SOUL

Poems and Inspirational

Writings for Spiritual and

Personal Growth

Volume One

## Tracey L. Moore

Oasis for My Soul: Poems and Inspirational Writings for Spiritual and Personal Growth

Unless otherwise noted, all Scripture quotations are from the King James Version of the Bible.

Scripture quotations marked (NIV) are taken from the Holy Bible, New International Version®, NIV®. Copyright © 1973, 1978, 1984, 2011 by Biblica, Inc.™ Used by permission of Zondervan. All rights reserved worldwide. www.zondervan.com, and the "NIV" and "New International Version" are trademarks registered in the United States Patent and Trademark Office by Biblica, Inc.™

Scripture quotations marked (AMP) are taken from the Amplified Bible, Copyright © 1954, 1958, 1962, 1964, 1965, 1987 by The Lockman Foundation. Used by permission.

ISBN: 978-1478394075

Cover Photo: Palm Tree in the Sahara (http://www.123rf.com)

Prepared for Publication by Tanya R. Liverman, Owner of Native Productions (http://www.nativeproductionva.com)

Edited by Cynthia Huffman

# CONTENTS

# ACKNOWLEDGMENTS

I would like to thank God first and foremost for helping me complete this project. He is my best friend, and I love Him so much. Lord, I thank and appreciate You for all the lessons You have taught me, and for the poems and inspirational messages that You downloaded to me as I walked with You daily. Thanks for ushering me into wholeness.

Thanks to my mom, Senie Moore, for her love, support and encouragement. Thank you for giving me life, taking me to church, and putting me in a position to be introduced to the Lord.

Thanks to my sister, Kimberly Cooper. You have been a great sounding board and tremendous support. You are so thorough, gracious, and capable, and I thank you for being willing to review my manuscript.

Thanks to my brother, Vincent Moore, who as an IT person helped me maintain my computer, which is an important tool in my writing endeavors.

Thanks to Bishop B. Courtney and Pastor Janeen McBath for being obedient to God and planting a church with an atmosphere that facilitates spiritual and personal growth. Bishop and Pastor, I want you to know how much I appreciate the rich Word, exhortation, and encouragement that you have poured into me on a weekly basis at Calvary Revival Church in Norfolk, Virginia.

Thanks to James Dowe, who always was willing to listen to me read my poetry and writings and encouraged me to be all that I could be. You have been such a positive person in my life, and I thank you for the constructive criticism you so lovingly gave and the ideas you gave me that I have incorporated into my work. Thanks for being a great friend and confidant.

Thanks to Judy Watson. I have appreciated your friendship, prayers and encouragement through the years.

Thanks to Kathy Crayton for being my friend and listening to me talk about my dreams and visions. You are a sweet and loving person with a good heart.

Thanks to Steve Williamson, who helped me make the quality decision to leave my job and pursue my dreams. Thanks for believing in me and telling me it was all going to work out. You changed my view of the world in a lot of ways. I appreciate your friendship.

Thanks to Veda Lassiter for holding me accountable for writing on a daily basis. You are my friend, and I appreciate your your listening ear.

Thanks to Jennifer Stewart, friend, fellow poet, writer, and dream chaser. Your willingness to follow your dream has inspired me to follow mine. We will get there.

Thanks to Tanya Liverman of Native Productions for your professionalism, your patience in walking me through this project, and your aid in bringing my dream to fruition.

Thanks to Cynthia Huffman for editing my book. I appreciate your expertise and skill, which definitely enhances my work.

And last, but certainly not least, thanks to you, the reader, for purchasing this book. Your support is so very much appreciated, and I pray that you will receive a spiritual blessing in return for the investment you have made.

# PROLOGUE

The first time I wrote a poem was in the third grade. Amazingly enough, I still remember it to this day, and it went like this:

> There is the Easter Bunny
> Coming down the street.
> Let's go and meet him,
> That just can't be beat!

Yes, it was kind of "cheesy," and I look back on it and laugh when I think about it. But what can you expect from a third-grader? Thank God, I have evolved poetically since those early years.

Today, I am all grown up, and I like to call myself The Purposeful Poet™ because when I write, I have an express purpose in mind. I do not seek to entertain, nor am I attempting to paint a picture with my words to move people emotionally. The poetry I present is not for the purpose of creative self-expression, because I want my work to be an expression of the heart of God. I endeavor to add value to people's lives through my poems, and to accomplish that desire, I must be inspired by the Holy Spirit. Unfortunately, people can't just come up to me and say, "Write a poem about XYZ," because if the Spirit doesn't download anything to me, I really have nothing to say. My ultimate purpose for writing is to challenge the reader to grow in some way, do something, or think differently after reading what I have written.

Sometimes when you read poetry, you may have to ponder deeply in order to discern the true meaning.

However, when you read each of the poems in this collection, know that you will easily discern what I am trying to convey because the poems are not "encrypted" in any way. My message will be clear and undeniable. I hope to challenge you and, sometimes, even make you uncomfortable. For in the state of discomfort, there is potential growth in Christ. Thus, my first goal is to help you to deepen your intimacy with God and encounter Him in a new way.

My second goal is for you to receive encouragement and comfort. We all need a little encouragement every now and then, don't we? Let's face it, life is not a picnic and, sooner or later, we will go through difficulties and hard times. Remember, Jesus said in John 16:33, "In the world, ye shall have tribulation." My hope is that the poems that you read will help to inspire you to trust God and finish your course—no matter what the devil throws at you.

My third goal is to address emotional issues that are a hindrance to your entering into a state of wholeness and knowing who you are in Christ. I want to help facilitate wholeness by challenging you to think about where you are in your journey toward emotional healing, and to help and encourage you, through the power of the Holy Spirit, to aggressively pursue wholeness. Becoming a whole person is vitally important to our being able to function effectively in our call so that we can fulfill the purpose that God has for us. Thus, these three objectives constitute the three-fold purpose of this literary work.

You may be wondering what prompted me to write *Oasis for My Soul, Volume One.* (This book is the first of two volumes.) Actually, I have been writing in my journal and seriously writing poetry since I started high school.

When I was inspired, I wrote sometimes on scraps of paper, napkins, or whatever I could get my hands on to capture an inspired thought. I just threw the writings in a file for years and forgot about them. Little did I know that God had a plan and would prompt me to pull the poems together and organize them into a collection years later. He was the One that orchestrated my departure from my job and lovingly freed me up so that I could pursue my dream of becoming a writer.

A little over a year ago, I was forced to leave my job due to health reasons. My job as a financial counselor at a major credit union had become so stressful that my blood pressure was dangerously high. However, it was normal, with medication, at home. When I went to the doctor, she told me she could not give me more medication because my blood pressure would go down too low at home, and I would likely end up passing out. She said, "It's your health," suggested that I get another job, and told me about another woman who ended up having a heart attack as a result of her hypertension issues. That was a wake-up call for me. A few years before, my dad had passed away as a result of a stroke, and I vowed that I would do everything in my power to avoid that. After much soul-searching and discussing the matter with family and friends, I decided it was time to go, and I resigned from my job with peace in my spirit.

Why did it take me so long to leave? I knew I'd leave at some point, but I didn't want to resign before God released me to do so. I thought, maybe the Lord had a lesson He wanted to teach me. Therefore, I did not want to leave too early and have to go through another similar circumstance to pass the test that He apparently had for me. I kept asking, "Lord, how will I know?" He faithfully orchestrated the circumstances so that it was as clear as a bell to me, and I learned the lesson of continuing on my journey and trusting God to make His will known to me as I moved forward. All I had to do was keep walking, and He eventually unfolded His plan to me in a way that was clear. I had the choice of staying and having my health ruined, or leaving and stepping out in faith onto nothingness. When it came to maintaining my health, I felt that there was no choice, so I left. I was free at last.

So, now what was I going to do with my life? I loved to write and often wrote in a devotional journal that I kept. I had a lot of creative ideas I wanted to pursue. I had inventions and games that I had thought of, but never had the time to attempt to bring them to fruition. One day, the idea came to me to organize all those scraps of paper that I had put in my poetry folder, and I began to type the poems into my computer. Then I said to myself, "Why not put together a collection of poems?" So that is what I set out to do.

A while back, I had an idea to write what I call a "poetic devotional," where I would write a poem and then explain the thought process and/or the situation out of which the poem had been birthed. I had never actually seen a poetry book like the one I had envisioned. I had seen the *Daily Bread* devotional wherein there was a little poem at the end of each daily entry to support the insight given within it. However, the concept of a poetry book with expository inspirational writings dispersed throughout was new to me. Furthermore, since I love to journal, I felt it would be a novel idea to write a poetry book that would cause the reader to interact with the poems and encourage people to think and grow spiritually through journaling.

Thus, I set out to write the book and decided to entitle it *Oasis for My Soul*. I chose this title because I pray that when you read the poems, they will refresh your spirit. If you are having a spiritual "dry spell," hopefully you will be able to read and absorb the poems and the inspirational writings that follow, and they will hydrate and nourish your soul. Ultimately, I hope that you will find a deeper, more satisfying relationship with the Master, Who is the true Oasis for our souls.

Since you have chosen to embark on this journey with me (and I am so very glad about that), I feel that it would be beneficial for you to receive an overview of the work. You will be reading thirty-one poems and inspirational writings that can be simply read as a poetry book or used as a book of daily devotional readings. Hopefully, you will be able to interact with the material and come to a better understanding of yourself, God, and others as you walk down the spiritually poetic trail that I have mapped out for you.

*Oasis for My Soul* is organized in such a way as to challenge you to think deeply about the poems that you read. After each poetic entry, there is an inspirationally written piece that will explain what prompted me to write the poem, my thoughts on the topic at hand, or perhaps a challenge to you, the reader, to think or act differently. Thought-provoking questions designed to help you apply the principles presented will follow the paragraphs expounding on the poem. Finally, each piece ends with a prayer where you will ask for the Father's help to grow spiritually and personally in various areas of your life. Therefore, you will be able to interact with the material you read and, hopefully, easily integrate the principles into your spiritual repertoire.

I want you to not only understand the message being conveyed and the underlying thought process that generated the poem, but also, perhaps, to come to a new level of spiritual awareness or even experience a paradigm shift. If you were inspired to make changes in your life that you feel you need to make, that would be thrilling to me. The bottom line is this: I do not want you to be the same after you read and reflect on what I feel the Lord gave me to share. Therefore, as you read, please keep a pen and notebook or journal handy. They will be useful as you read, reflect, and answer the questions that follow each poem.

It is my greatest desire that you enjoy the poems I have written, that they will quench your spiritual thirst and draw you a little closer to our Heavenly Father in some way. I pray that, even after you finish the book, if you run into a situation that is difficult, you will be able to pull the book off of the shelf, use the index to find the appropriate poem, and use this as a reference that will inspire and encourage you whenever you need it. I would love it if you find a poem or two that you want to share with someone who is dealing with a difficult issue covered in one of the chapters. May God bless you as you read this work. May He speak to your heart, and may your mind be renewed. May He cause you to take action when necessary, make wise choices, and be the best that you can be for Christ. I pray that you will enjoy the spiritual journey and emerge from it a better, stronger, more peaceful you.

# CHAPTER ONE

❦❦❦❦❦❦❦❦

# LOVE LETTERS TO GOD

❦❦❦❦❦❦❦❦

These entries have been written to praise and glorify God. The poems give honor to the King of Kings and are given first position in the book because God should rightfully have first place in everything. I pray that after reading them, your intimacy and personal relationship with the Father will be enhanced.

You must strive to be continuously aware of God's divine presence. He is able to keep you and assist you in whatever you are facing moment by moment.

## I ENJOY YOUR COMPANY

*I enjoy your company, Dear God,*
*I love spending time with You.*
*It's like sitting and talking to an old friend*
*Who knows me through and through.*
*I tell You all about my cares,*
*And You listen attentively.*
*Then the timely Word You speak*
*Puts it all in perspective for me.*
*Who could ask for a better friend?*
*You're a wonderful person to know.*
*You're loving, caring, gentle and kind,*
*And that's why I love You so.*
*I want to fellowship with You,*
*It's Your face that I seek, not Your hand.*
*I don't want to forget about You when*
*I've reached my Promised Land.*
*I can sit in Your presence and not say a word,*
*I bask in the warmth of Your light.*
*I find comfort in Your loving arms,*
*I know everything will be alright.*
*I genuinely enjoy You,*
*Your friendship is my delight.*
*I've got to connect with You each day,*
*Or I simply don't feel right.*
*Lord, I want to know You better,*
*For You mean the world to me.*
*I long to sit at Your feet because*
*I enjoy Your company.*

> You have made known to me the path of life;
> you will fill me with joy in your presence,
> with eternal pleasures at your right hand.
> **Psalm 16:11 (NIV)**

Joyce Meyer, one of my favorite authors, has said that when we spend time with God, we should "seek His face and not His hand."[1] What she means is that when we meet with God, our focus should not always be on obtaining something from Him. Instead, we need to be satisfied just to be in His presence.

Many times, I have been in the presence of God and ended up making it a monologue. That is, I did all the talking and God did all the listening. I did not give Him the opportunity to get a word in edgewise. It was all about me. Finally, I came to the conclusion that maybe God had something important that He wanted to say. I just needed to take the time to listen.

My time with God is much more enjoyable when I dialogue with Him. One of the things that I love to do is sit in my easy chair and pull out my journal. Next, I write in my journal, "Speak Lord, Your servant is listening," as stated in Samuel 3:9 (NIV). Then I wait. Next, I write down whatever comes to mind, and receive that as what the Lord is saying to me. Thus, He is writing through my own hand what He wants to communicate. I have gotten so many breakthroughs in my thinking this way. I bring a situation before God that I am struggling with by writing down a brief summary of what I am experiencing, and then write down what He is saying to me about it. As I write, He identifies errors in my thinking that are causing me emotional pain. Sometimes He will just tell me how much

He loves me and how important it is for me to trust Him during the difficult time I am going through. Other times, He sends me to books on my shelf and pinpoints passages that I need to revisit. Sometimes He brings a scripture to mind; I look it up, and the Spirit expounds upon it and gives me revelation. The times with God where both of us are able to speak are the richest and most enjoyable times that I have with Him.

Having an intimate, one-on-one relationship with the Father is a wonderful experience. To know Him is to love Him. Some people may say, "How can you sit in a room by yourself and enjoy a person you can't even see or hear them speak audibly?" My answer is this: Try it, you will like it. If you know Jesus as your personal Savior, ask God to reveal Himself to you in a new way. Tell Him that you sincerely desire to know Him better, and discover what it's like to enjoy His company on a deeper level. Begin to spend time with Him regularly, make yourself available and, trust me, you will develop an intimacy with God like never before. You will be able to say with a smile on your face, "Lord, I sure do enjoy Your company." And He will say to you, "I enjoy your company, too, My child."

## REFLECTION

1. Take ten minutes and just sit in the presence of God. Do not say a word. Just get quiet. Relax in the Lord. After the ten minutes is up, write about the experience in your journal.

2. Try writing down this phrase spoken by young Samuel in I Samuel 3:9 (NIV): "Speak, Lord, Your servant is listening." Then write down whatever comes to your mind.

## PRAYER

God, I thank You for making Yourself available to me 24 hours a day, seven days a week. Although sometimes I have many cares, I don't want You to feel that I only want to spend time with You because of what You can do for me. I am sorry if I have made You feel that way. My desire, O Lord, is to bask in Your presence and get to know You on a deeper, more intimate level. I know that it is in that secret place where we meet daily that You communicate to me and change me incrementally. Please empower me to make the right choices in my life so that I make You a priority. Let me get to know You better in all of Your glory. I pray for us to enjoy sweet fellowship as we come together to talk each day. Please enable me to develop a new and deeper level of intimacy with You that I have not experienced before. In Jesus' name I pray, amen.

## *AWESOME ARE YOU*

*Awesome are You, Lord of all grace,*

*No one else can take Your place.*

*Early in the morning I seek Your face,*

*So that I may better run my race.*

*Thank You, Lord, for bringing me out,*

*Around Jericho's wall I gave my shout.*

*A massive stronghold came tumbling down,*

*A brand new freedom I have found.*

*Awesome are You, my God.*

You are awesome, O God, in your sanctuary;
the God of Israel gives power and strength
to his people. Praise be to God!
Psalm 68:35 (NIV)

Our God is truly awesome. Think of how He assembled the solar system. All of the planets orbit the sun and turn on their individual axes without crashing into each other. How phenomenal is that?! Look at our bodies. They are machines that have been engineered with such intricate detail. Who in their right mind would think that there could not be a Master Designer behind all of this? Take the ecosystem. God designed things so that we breathe out the carbon dioxide that the plants need to live. Plants, in turn, expel the oxygen that we need to live and breathe. How brilliant is that?!

Another reason God is awesome is that He engineered the plan of salvation. He knew that we would need a Savior, so He came up with a plan that would allow Him to fellowship with us even though He is holy and righteous and we are not. The plan allowed people of any race, creed, color, intellect, social class, and socioeconomic background to receive Jesus as Savior and Lord. Salvation is a free gift to whosoever will come to God and believe that Jesus died on the cross and rose from the dead.

Yes, we serve an awesome God. When we reflect on His awesomeness, it helps us to embrace and believe in His omnipotence. Let us acknowledge His greatness on a daily basis. He truly deserves all of the praise and glory forevermore. Amen.

## REFLECTION

1. Take time to list the attributes of God that make Him awesome to you. This does not include what He has done for you. Specifically list the qualities about God that make Him special to you.

2. Now, what awesome things has He done for you lately?

## PRAYER

Lord, You are truly an awesome wonder! I give You praise. I exalt and extol You. I give glory to Your awesome name. I worship You for who You are. I lift my voice to honor You. I refuse to let the rocks cry out for me. I bless Your holy and awesome name. Father, let me be more frequently aware of Your presence, Your power, and Your attributes as I give You glory through my daily living. I love You, God. In Jesus' name I pray, amen.

## ALL THAT I NEED

*Loves me so sweetly,*
*Accepts so completely,*
*Meets every one of my needs.*
*All the way for me,*
*Prepares the way for me,*
*My Father is awesome, indeed.*
*Loves me so deeply,*
*He cares so uniquely,*
*He has my best interests at heart.*
*Approves of me greatly,*
*I'm more aware lately*
*Of love He so freely imparts.*
*Some people are fickle,*
*They're not worth a nickel,*
*They won't stay through the thick and thin.*
*They will turn upon you,*
*Not remembering who*
*Forgave them of all of their sin.*
*But the Lord is not so,*
*And I won't fear my foes,*
*For my God will never leave me.*
*When the saints do withdraw*
*'Cause I've broken their "law,"*
*God is faithful, His grace I will see.*
*God offers so much,*
*And I live for His touch,*
*He'll comfort when everyone leaves.*
*I'll not be alone,*
*God is still on His throne,*
*He surely is all that I need.*

[B]e content with what you have, because
God has said, "Never will I leave you; never will
I forsake you." So we may say with confidence,
"The Lord is my helper; I will not be afraid.
What can man do to me?"
Hebrews 13:5-6 (NIV)

We all have had a fear of loss at one time or another: the fear of losing a job, the fear of losing or not having any money, the fear of losing a loved one or a love interest. However, we need to understand that no matter what we lose in this life, Jesus is truly all that we need. When we get to the place where we recognize this life-changing truth, those fears will dissipate into thin air.

In Psalm 46:2, David writes, "Therefore will not we fear, though the earth be removed and though the mountains be carried into the midst of the sea; Though the waters thereof roar and be troubled, though the mountains shake with the swelling thereof. Selah." You see, when you have Jesus, it doesn't matter what happens to you from day to day. When "the mountains fall into the sea" and everything falls apart, you can be assured that Jesus will never leave you or forsake you. In Him, you have all you need to rebuild, for He promised in Matthew 6:33 that He will add everything that you need unto you if you will just seek His Kingdom first.

Jesus is really all that we need because, in His Word, He promised to provide for us and, because we are His children, He has taken responsibility for us and our well-being. Therefore, if you are connected to God through His Son, you will always have your need met by the Almighty Creator of the Universe Himself. He is your provider, and you have access to all of the resources of God because He owns everything, including the cattle on a thousand hills (Psalm 50:10). Because of the vast supply of resources that belong to Him and His promise to supply all of the needs of His children, there is absolutely no need to fear lack. We must simply pray, have faith, speak the Word, and seek His Kingdom first, then watch God perform His Word.

Another issue that we sometimes get confused about is the need for certain people in our lives. People will come and go, but Jesus is a constant; He always stays the same (Hebrews 13:8). We don't have to guess whether Jesus will be there for us. He will. Therefore, when it comes to our need for people, He really is all that we need. He created us to be relational beings, and when we stay in connection with Him, He will orchestrate divine connections for us. He wants us to have fellowship with others, and He will supply that need via a physical human presence or His divine spiritual presence when necessary.

This may seem a little crazy, but it's true. I am single, and I remember lying in bed one night and telling God, "I sure do need a hug, and I don't even have anybody to give me one." He told me, "I'll give you a hug." At that moment, I felt his presence envelop me and a warm feeling come over me. God had given me a hug. So even when you may not have someone physically present, God can still meet your need in a special way.

To summarize, it is so important that we remember these truths: 1) No matter what other people do, or what happens to us in this life, God has promised that He will be faithful to us; 2) He said He would be with us even until the end of the age (Matthew 28:20); and 3) He would supply every need if we prioritize His Kingdom (Philippians 4:19).

Isn't it comforting to know that the Almighty God will never forsake us, reject us, or let us down? Know in your heart that God will sustain you and keep you company even in your darkest moments. He is the Great I AM, He will be what you need Him to be in the now, and He absolutely is all that you need.

## REFLECTION

1. Can you think of any areas in your life where you fear that your needs will not be met? Write them down. If you have had fears in the past, how have you dealt with them?

2. Do you have anyone in your life right now who causes you to feel that you would not be able to make it or you would not be able to be happy if that person was removed from your life? Ask the Holy Spirit to help you identify that person.

3. Do you have anything in your life right now that causes you to feel that you would not be able to make it or you would not be able to be happy if that item was taken away? Ask the Holy Spirit to reveal it to you if necessary.

4. If you were able to identify a fear, person, or thing, please take time to reflect and talk to God about it and ask Him what He would have you to do. Write down what comes to mind in your journal.

## PRAYER

Dear God, I want You to always be the center of my world. Help me build my life around You. Let my joy be in You alone. You are my Rock. Thank You for stabilizing my life. I depend on You, and I need You desperately. Thank You for meeting every single need that I have. You are my Shepherd, and I shall not want (Psalm 23). Please help me to know deep down in my sanctified soul that everything I need is found in You. In Jesus' name I pray, amen.

## OASIS FOR MY SOUL

*Your Love is an Oasis for my thirsty soul.*
*I drink from the pool of Your refreshing Love.*
*You hydrate my spirit, and pour into me*
*Your liquid Love.*
*I thirstily drink more and more;*
*But my thirst for Your Love is never quenched.*
*I must continually drink from*
*the Oasis every single day I live.*
*It satisfies and refreshes like nothing else can.*
*I immerse myself in the Oasis of Your Love.*
*There, I find Living Water.*
*I am so thankful for Your Love that engulfs me*
*and permeates my very being.*
*When all around is an arid desert,*
*in a world that is so void of Love,*
*Your Love is a cool, refreshing drink*
*in a dry and thirsty land.*
*You, O God, are the Oasis for my soul.*

"God, thou art my God; early will I seek thee: my
soul thirsteth for thee, my flesh longeth for thee
in a dry and thirsty land, where no water is."
Psalm 63:1

There is so much that we go through on a day-to-day
basis in the course of living. As we deal with the world and
all that it entails, we can sometimes fail to spend as much
time with God as we need to. The "busyness" in our lives
causes us to miss our time with God, and He ends up being
"put on the back burner." When we neglect Him in that
manner, it's to our own detriment, not His.

In the natural order of things, water is essential, yet
there may be times when we will go for several days
without stopping to drink from the well of Living Water.
When we take time to spend time with God and fellowship
with the Holy Spirit, it's as if we are drinking supernatural
water that quenches the thirst in our soul. When we
experience His loving presence, it's like being filled up with
refreshing pure water that hydrates our spirit.

How do we know that our soul is thirsty? How do we
know that our spirit is parched? In *Merriam-Webster's
Collegiate® Dictionary*, the definition of dehydration is
"...an abnormal depletion of ... fluids."[2] In Ephesians 5:26
we see that the Word is likened unto water. When we are
spiritually dehydrated, we can easily tell that we have "lost
water" because the Word is far from our lips. The Word
does not instantly come to our minds when needed. We
encounter situations, and we fail to apply the principles of
the Word, because we have not had a "drink" in a long time.
When we are parched, we may feel unloved. We may feel

ungrateful and fail to count the blessings God has given us. Our relationships suffer because we fail to apply the Living Water of the Word to our daily encounters with others. A thirsty, dehydrated soul loses its sense of joy, and spiritual weakness is sure to follow (Nehemiah 8:10).

We must realize that sitting in church and listening to a sermon once per week for fifteen minutes to an hour is not enough. Just as one glass of water per week is not enough, we must drink from the well of the Holy Ghost on a daily basis. We must bask in the presence of the Lord and let Him saturate us with His love and thoughts. For when we feel His love, and His thoughts replace our thoughts, then our soul and spirit will be thoroughly hydrated and we will be able to function effectively in His Kingdom, even if the world in which we live is like an arid desert. God can truly be the Oasis for us in the midst of it all.

## REFLECTION

1. What, if anything, is the Holy Spirit saying to you in regard to the "hydration" of your soul and spirit, and what action do you need to take?

2. Are there any obstacles that are keeping you from getting a regular quiet time with God? If so, what are they, and what is your strategy for overcoming them?

## PRAYER

Lord, I need You. Forgive me when I allow myself to be drawn away from the well of Your Spirit. Please help me to not allow the "busyness" of daily living to keep me from drinking of Your Living Water on a daily basis. Let me not even feel comfortable without stopping to spend time with You each day and allowing You to hydrate my spirit. Help me glorify You and represent You well in this earth. Thank You for loving me as You do. In Jesus' name I pray, amen.

# CHAPTER TWO

# JOURNEY INTO WHOLENESS

As I walked through my journey toward wholeness, God taught me lessons that I have written into these poems. When I was able to write a poem about a lesson that God may have been trying to teach me for years, it was a clue to me that I was finally "getting it." That was indicative of my progress, and writing the poems out on paper was healing for me in a sense. I hope that as you read them, you will move closer to becoming whole. These poems are designed to build self-esteem and challenge negative "thought bombs" that the enemy has continuously dropped in our minds, even since childhood.

God has ascribed infinite value and worth to us, but unless we recognize and accept His valuation, we will never experience abundant living.

## *FEARFULLY AND WONDERFULLY MADE*

*You made me what You want me to be*
*To do what You called me to do,*
*You had a purpose in mind for me,*
*Lord, I was made for You.*
*I am an artistic masterpiece,*
*An expression of Your heart,*
*Master, I am Your workmanship.*
*I am a breed apart.*
*There'll never be another like me,*
*Nor will I be like another,*
*That was never Your intent for me,*
*Through Your Word I have discovered*
*That I am unique, and that is why*
*This personality,*
*Was placed in my soul by You, Oh God,*
*Oh, so deliberately.*
*You envisioned what You desired to create,*
*And then You set to work,*
*You skillfully and artfully fashioned me,*
*Then set the stage for my birth.*
*You made me the way that I am,*
*Your mission I must fulfill,*
*I'm so glad that You made me thus,*
*So that I may accomplish Your will.*
*I am an arrow in Your hand,*
*A stone in Your sling to be hurled,*
*A weapon to be used by You, my King,*
*I was made to impact this world.*
*I praise You, I'm fearfully and wonderfully made,*
*Your works are quite wondrous it's true,*
*You said, "It is good," when You finished Your work,*
*And I'm in agreement with You.*

**"I will praise thee; for I am fearfully and
wonderfully made: marvelous are thy works;
and that my soul knoweth right well."
Psalm 139:14**

God is a Master Craftsman, and David recognized that in Psalm 134. Some may say that his words reek of arrogance. But when the verse is examined, we find that the operative phrase is "I will praise thee." When we preface an acknowledgement of our positive attributes with sincere praise to our God, there is nothing wrong with that. I know that God appreciates our praise.

However, some of us will never say anything positive about ourselves. We are quick to point out all of our flaws, but hesitant to acknowledge the treasure, gifts and talents that God has deposited in us. We believe that if we talk about our positive qualities, that is pride. That is what the devil wants us to think. It is true that Proverbs 27:2 states, "Let another man praise thee, and not thine own mouth; a stranger, and not thine own lips." Therefore, we should not go around bragging to everyone about how great we are. That is definitely not humility. Humility recognizes and acknowledges our good qualities that God gave to us, and then we take the time to give Him praise for them.

We must make a pact with ourselves and purpose in our hearts to never make negative comments to ourselves or about ourselves. God fearfully and wonderfully made us all. Ephesians 2:10 states, "For we are his workmanship, created in Christ Jesus unto good works." That means that we are His artwork. We are all unique masterpieces created by God Himself.

Imagine that you are attending an art show at a museum where a local artist is displaying his work. You notice that the artist is present and standing by a sculpture that he created. You walk over, and he begins to tell you what his thought processes were when he created the piece. The tone of his presentation indicates a sense of pride in his work. After he finishes the explanation of his work, you say to him, "I really think that's ugly. It doesn't speak to me at all." Would you actually say something like that?! Most of us would never do that, yet we will say negative, hurtful things about ourselves, and insult God in the process.

From this point forward, be determined that you will only say positive things about yourself, the artwork of God. Give Him praise for your positive attributes. Thank Him for the person that He created you to be, and remember that which was written in Genesis 1:31: "And God saw every thing that he had made, and, behold, it was very good."

## REFLECTION

1. Think about how your day has gone so far. Have you said or thought anything negative about yourself? Write down those things that you said or thought.

2. Would you say those things to a friend? What would you have said to a friend?

3. What do you think God thinks or feels about what you said or thought about yourself?

## PRAYER

Dear God, I praise You for I am fearfully and wonderfully made. Thank You for the thought and care that You put into making me, Your servant. Please help me recognize and acknowledge Your handiwork and give You the praise. Help me be quick to say good things about myself in the same way that I encourage others. Holy Spirit, please bring it to my attention when I speak negatively about myself and empower me to speak words of life instead. Thank You for helping me renew my mind in this area. In Jesus' name I pray, amen.

## *ACCEPTABLE*

*If you never read another self-help book,*
*Never journal another page,*
*Never go to another counseling session,*
*Or fast another day,*
*If you don't pray every single day,*
*To church you never go,*
*You stop trying to please other people,*
*But Jesus Christ you know,*
*If you never get to marry,*
*If you don't have any friends,*
*Not one soul likes you in this world,*
*With your family you're not "in,"*
*You are acceptable the way you are*
*Because God gave up His best,*
*Because of what Jesus did on the cross,*
*You have God's righteousness.*
*It's not about the things you do,*
*But it's all in Who you know.*
*Because Jesus sacrificed His life,*
*Know that you're good to go.*
*God accepts you exactly as you are,*
*Right here, right now, it's true.*
*There's no need to reject yourself,*
*He has infinite love for you.*
*He knows that you're not perfect,*
*He knows your thoughts from afar,*
*He knows your frame, that you are dust,*
*So accept YOU the way you are.*

"Who has bewitched you? ... Are you so foolish?
After beginning with the Spirit, are you now
trying to attain your goal by human effort?"
Galatians 3:1-3 (NIV)

When God saved us, we came to Him just as we were. He accepted us right where we were. The only thing God required in order for us to be saved was faith. We believed that Jesus died on the cross to pay the penalty for our sins and rose from the dead. Because of that alone, God credited our faith as righteousness (Romans 4). Wrapped in Christ, we are viewed by God as acceptable and righteous.

Even as Christians, sometimes it is so hard for us to accept ourselves. None of us is perfect, yet we still think that we have to DO something to be OK. We use all sorts of counterfeit standards to establish our own sense of righteousness and be able to judge ourselves as acceptable. But God says to us that the sacrifice of His Son is enough. Period.

The truth is that we can't earn our righteousness through our works. It is a free gift, but our works should be the evidence of our faith (James 2:18). Thus, our salvation began with a spiritual emphasis in that we were made righteous by a divine exchange, not through works of the flesh. In II Corinthians 5:21, Paul writes, "God made him who had no sin to be sin for us, so that in him we might become the righteousness of God." Somewhere along the line, we got it twisted and believed that we had to perform or meet certain self-imposed standards in order to gain and maintain our righteousness, and be acceptable to ourselves, others, and God. God has declared to us that we are "accepted in the beloved" (Ephesians 1:6) just as we are. Righteousness has been imputed to all who believe.

Now, this may sound silly, but one of the reasons I found it hard to accept God's gift of righteousness was because I was afraid that if I accepted myself as righteous by God's standard (accepting Jesus Christ as my Savior), I would be lax when it came to sin. If I didn't beat myself up, then I would really act out! I had to whip myself into shape. Therefore, righteousness did not compute for me. However, Paul addressed this in Romans 6:1-2 when he wrote, "What shall we say then? Shall we continue in sin, so that grace may abound? God forbid. How shall we, that are dead to sin, live any longer therein?" So, just because grace has been extended to us does not mean we can live any way that we want. If we really love God, we will want to keep His commandments (John 14:21), and He will put a desire in us to do what He commands (Hebrews 8:10).

Therefore, today, we need to recognize that our own works will not suffice in making us acceptable because, in Christ, we already are acceptable despite all our flaws and weaknesses. Most of us were not brought up to believe this. It seems too simple, just too good to be true. In our minds we must behave perfectly, have all our ducks in a row, be all things to all people, never let others see our weaknesses, and be a superhero in order to feel OK about ourselves. But God has spoken. Know that in Christ, you are completely and totally acceptable. You are OK. Now let that sink in, and then exhale.

## REFLECTION

1. Is there any situation that has happened lately to cause you to feel "not OK" about yourself? What was the circumstance?

2. As you reflect on that situation, ask the Holy Spirit to reveal the truth to you about any errors in your thinking. Write down what comes to mind now and in the coming days.

3. What have you done lately in an effort to make yourself feel acceptable and OK in your own mind? Ask the Holy Spirit to help you identify "the works of the flesh" in your own life.

4. In light of what you have read, what changes in your thinking are necessary so that you see things from God's perspective?

## PRAYER

Dear God, I repent of trying to establish my own righteousness through my own fruitless works. I see now that my belief that Jesus died on the cross for my sins and rose from the dead is all that is necessary for me to be acceptable and righteous in Your sight. Please drive that truth deep into the recesses of my heart by Your Spirit. Thank You for accepting me just as I am and helping me feel OK about myself in spite of my weaknesses and shortcomings. In Jesus' name I pray, amen.

### I'M WHO GOD SAYS I AM

*I am God's child, I am in Christ;*
*I'm who God says I am.*
*No matter what the circumstance,*
*I answer to the Lamb.*
*Because of my belief in Him,*
*I have His righteousness.*
*I am OK, and I'm on my way[3]*
*To wholeness, I'm truly blessed.*
*Others may judge and reject me,*
*They may not recognize*
*The gifts and talents God gave to me,*
*But my value's still "supersized."*
*It's not about their whims and views;*
*People may judge my worth.*
*But God filled me with His treasure*
*Before He predestined my birth.*
*My self-esteem took a beating,*
*But now I've got a grip.*
*Satan can't take me back down that road;*
*I refuse to go on that trip.*
*I know that God has established my worth,*
*I was blind, but now I see.*
*I am only who my God says I am,*
*And I'll be all He wants me to be.*

## "Who told you that you were naked?"
## Genesis 3:11 (NIV)

A child develops his self-image based on what others convey to him through words and actions. I am sure that you have had messages relayed to you by the words or deeds of people who were supposed to be in your corner but weren't. In spite of what anyone has ever said to you or how they have treated you, God is saying that only what He says about you is the truth. Only He can tell you who you are and what you can do, because He is your Creator. The enemy is on a mission to annihilate your self-esteem and make you loathe yourself to the point where you can't function in the call that God has upon your life. Satan's chief goal is to make you miss your destiny.

You must come to the place where you see yourself the way God sees you. You must not automatically accept what others say about you as truth. Instead, purpose to ask the Holy Spirit what truth is, believe the Word of the Lord, and decide how you will view yourself based on that. Otherwise, you are destined for misery.

Because sin entered the world, and we have had the enemy lie to us since birth, our view of ourselves and of the world is inaccurate. Our vision of ourselves has become unclear and faulty, and we need to wear "glasses" with "spiritual lenses" to perceive ourselves and the world accurately. If we let him, the devil will give us any old pair of reading glasses to put on that come from "Hell's Drugstore" that we were never meant to wear. He'll say to us, "Here, wear these." If we take them and put them on, we will still see ourselves according to what people have told us. We will have a distorted view of ourselves.

When we got saved, God said, "Come over here and sit in my Divine Optometrist chair." He made us look through the machine and flipped the lenses around until we could see clearly. He gave us glasses with prescription lenses in Christ so that we could see ourselves as righteous and see the world around us from a basis of reality rather than what others tell us. When we look through the lenses that we were meant to wear, we see ourselves and the world as we should.

All day long, the devil tries to tell you who you are through the people and circumstances around you. You must know what the Word of God says about you, and grasp the truth of that in the core of your being. Remember that in His Word, God has told you exactly who you are. Your job is to ignore all information that you receive that is contrary to what He has said, and walk into your destiny.

## REFLECTION

1. What lies have people told you in your life that conflict with the Word of God?

2. What scriptures can you find in the Word of God to refute those lies?

## PRAYER

Dear Lord, I thank You for the truth of Your Word. I have been told many lies about myself in this life by the accuser of the brethren (Revelations 12:10). Please help me identify any lies that the enemy has told me through people and circumstances. Enable me to uproot those lies and replace them with Your Word. May Your Holy Spirit guide me into all truth about the real me. In Jesus' name I pray, amen.

## MY VALENTINE

*You are My Valentine, My love, My cherished one.*
*My awesome creation, My beautiful child,*
*You are fearfully and wonderfully made.*
*You're the apple of My eye.*
*You are My marvelous work,*
*My workmanship forged to do My bidding*
*and make a difference in this world.*
*As My love is poured out to you,*
*you will pour out My love to others.*
*You will glorify Me.*
*You are My heart.*
*You are My Valentine.*

## "I am my beloved's, and my beloved is mine."
## Song of Solomon 6:3

God wants you to grasp the depth, breadth, and height of His love for you. For when you know how much He loves you, there is no need to fear anything. Perfect love casts out all fear (I John 4:18). Think about that. Your Father loves you perfectly. If His love for you is perfect, then that means that you can trust Him fully. He has nothing but good intentions toward you. He will be fiercely protective of you, and because He is omnipotent, you know that He controls the universe. Therefore, He will definitely keep you safe.

Today, your heavenly Father wants you to feel His love radiating toward you. But even when you can't feel it, know that it's there. Just as when the clouds cover the sun and we cannot see its rays, we know that does not mean the sun ceases to shine. Even when we visit the beach on a cloudy day, we can still get sunburn from the ultraviolet rays of the sun that penetrate the clouds. Likewise, even when you can't feel God's love, know that His love covers you and is from everlasting to everlasting. It never ceases no matter what you do or don't do. How awesome is that?

Because God sent His Son to die for you, that is the ultimate evidence of His love. Know that you are in His thoughts (Jeremiah 29:11), and your image is engraved on the palm of His hand according to Isaiah 49:16 (NIV). You are His, and He is yours. Nothing can ever change that. You are Valentines by covenant, forever.

## REFLECTION

1. Was there ever a time when you doubted God's love for you? What was happening at that time?

2. Write about a time when you felt overwhelmed by God's love.

3. What are your thoughts about God's love for you at this moment based on what you read above?

## PRAYER

Dear God, I love you very much. Even when I don't always feel Your presence or Your love, help me believe the truth of Your Word, which says that You love me with an everlasting love (Jeremiah 31:3). During difficult times, let the knowledge of Your love for me sustain me and give me hope. Let me be secure in the knowledge that You love me unconditionally and that Your love for me will never change. You love me maximally at this moment and for all time, and for that I am grateful. In Jesus' name I pray, amen.

## THE SACRED SPACE

*Inside myself there is a space*
*That no one else can touch,*
*Whatever people say or do,*
*It doesn't matter much.*
*For in that space exists a child,*
*The true "me," good as gold.*
*They may abuse my body,*
*But they'll never touch my soul.*
*Satan may play his mind games*
*And break my heart again,*
*But my Sacred Space is still intact,*
*I'll never let him win.*
*I'm the temple of the living God,*
*His home is my Sacred Space,*
*The Holy Spirit indwells me,*
*No one else can enter this place.*
*For what I show outside myself*
*Is merely what they see,*
*Underneath this mask and all the pain*
*There's a hidden part of me.*

**"Know ye not that your body is the temple
of the Holy Ghost which is in you, which
ye have of God, and ye are not your own?"
I Corinthians 6:19**

Inside every one of us is a place I call the "Sacred Space" that is the very core of our being. There are three things that are found in this safe haven. First of all, our true self is housed in the Sacred Space. Everyone can see our fleshly bodies, but that is not really who we are. Our spirit (with a little "s"), the real person we are, is hidden in there.

Secondly, the Sacred Space is the place within us where the Spirit of God (with a big "S") dwells. The Word tells us in I Corinthians 3:16-17 that our bodies are the temple of the Holy Spirit, which means we are the dwelling place of Almighty God. Selah. (What an awesome revelation!) So this Sacred Space is where His Spirit interacts with our spirit and enables Him to speak to us and guide us through this life.

Thirdly, the Sacred Space is the place where our true value and worth lies. Our value is constant and stable, and has been declared by God in Psalm 49:8 (NIV), which relays, "The ransom for a life is costly, and no payment is ever enough." This confirms the fact that God views us, His creation, as infinitely valuable to Him and that He has deposited treasure of infinite measure inside these earthen vessels of ours.

I like to think that the Sacred Space in our bodies is like the "safe room" in a house. The safe room is a fortified room where a family can go if a hurricane hits or other hazardous weather conditions prevail. Even if the whole house is blown away, the safe room will be more likely to stand. It's an area in the home where the family can be safe from harm and danger. We, too, have a "safe room" in our "house." It's a place within us where our spirit, God's Spirit, and our true value are walled off and cannot be accessed or compromised. Thus, the Sacred Space that is in our bodies, like a safe room, provides a place of safety and refuge.

Therefore, it doesn't matter what happens outside of us because our Sacred Space will always be intact. God is always with us, and greater is He that lives in us, than he that is in this world (I John 4:4). Our regenerated spirit, that perfect part of us that became alive when we accepted Christ as our Savior, will always be protected in there. Our worth and value are secure and constant, and the potential to become all God wants us to be is still in there. It cannot be touched, for it is locked away for safekeeping with the Master. Even if we sin and our performance is imperfect, even if the world's perception of us is less than stellar, our spirit is perfect and God has declared that we are the righteousness of God in Christ. Therefore, we can love and feel good about ourselves in spite of anything that may be going on externally.

Because of these truths, whenever there is a storm that is raging in our lives, we know we can go to the "safe room" and find tranquility and shelter there. Psalm 61:3 says this of God: "[T]hou hast been a shelter for me, and a strong tower from the enemy." The Sacred Space is the place where our born-again spirit connects with God's Spirit, where we can hear from Him and find joy in His presence, comfort for our souls, and peace and security in knowing that He loves us. We can be reminded of our true worth and value, regardless of what man thinks of us or how badly we've failed. It's a space where we can crawl up into our Heavenly Father's lap in the spirit, feel His embrace, and hear Him say, "All is well; you are safe, My child." It's at that moment we feel that we have truly found a shelter from the storm in the Sacred Space.

## REFLECTION

1. How can you use the awareness of the Sacred Space to help you maintain your sense of righteousness when your behavior is less than perfect?

2. How does the knowledge of the Sacred Space help you understand your true worth and value and keep you from allowing the enemy to cause you to feel less valuable than God has declared you to be?

3. How can you use the awareness of the Sacred Space to help you handle the storms of life?

## PRAYER

Dear God, thank You for the Sacred Space that You placed within me. Please help me to always remember beyond a shadow of a doubt how You have instilled me with innate worth and value, and I pray that I will never let myself be convinced otherwise by anything that others say or do. I declare that I am firmly rooted and grounded in Your Word, and I am thoroughly equipped to handle the storms of life that will inevitably come my way because You reside in me and provide a refuge for me. I thank You that my spirit within is perfect, Jesus' blood covers me, and I am the righteousness of God in Christ. I ask that You continue to do whatever it takes to make me whole in every single area of my life. In Jesus' name I pray, amen.

## THE BREAKING OF A STRONGHOLD

*The devil had his way for years,*
*Yes, Satan, you had me bound,*
*But I'm here to declare in Jesus' name*
*This stronghold has come down!*
*My mind was twisted and in a fog,*
*Deception was rampant in me,*
*But God intervened and saved the day,*
*The Lord has set me free.*
*My soul is set free from the fowler's snare,*
*My thoughts taken captive, you see,*
*To the obedience of Jesus, my Savior and King,*
*Satan has no control over me.*
*Imaginations have been tamed,*
*A new peace I now have found,*
*I praise God's name and give Him thanks,*
*This stronghold has come down!*
*The weapons used could not be seen,*
*The battle was fierce and long,*
*The stronghold has been broken, thank God,*
*In my heart there is now a song.*

> "For the weapons of our warfare are
> not carnal, but mighty through God
> to the pulling down of strongholds."
> II Corinthians 10:4

What is a stronghold? The definition of a stronghold according to *Merriam-Webster's Collegiate® Dictionary* is "a fortified place; ... a place dominated by a particular group...."[4] Therefore, a stronghold is a place in our minds that is dominated by Satan. He sets up a fortified place in our minds, a lie or a wrong way of thinking that has become deeply rooted. It is a tightly held belief or a habitual way of thinking that is difficult to dispel.

How is a stronghold developed? It starts out as a lie planted in our minds directly by Satan or through those around us. A family member, friend, bully, or teacher says something negative or hurtful to us, and we feel emotional pain. Satan uses that opportunity to inject a lie into our psyche. Once the lie is planted, it is further watered and fertilized by other people saying things to reinforce the untruth, or by circumstances that support it. We continue to believe it more and more until it is a reality for us. At that point, it is officially classified as a stronghold.

How is a stronghold broken? The first step to breaking a stronghold is to identify it by comparing the renegade belief to the truth of God's Word. However, if we don't know the Word of God, it will be impossible to identify. Once we identify a stronghold we must take the thought captive according to II Corinthians 10:5. How do we take a thought captive? There are several ways that we can do this, but it will not happen overnight. It is a continuous process. We have to challenge the renegade thought over and over again until it finally gives way to truth. This takes time and consistency in bombarding the lie with the truth of God's Word. We must spend time with God every day, target the area where the untruth has been identified, and hold it up to the light of the Word. That means finding scriptures that deal with that issue and committing them to memory, or writing them over and over. Another way to take the thought captive is to develop confessions that incorporate the Word of God and declare exactly what we want to happen in our lives, write them down, and say them aloud daily. Additionally, we can keep a journal, listen, and wait for God to speak to us, then write down whatever He says.

There are other important weapons we can use to demolish strongholds. Regular fasting and prayer are necessities. We must pray without ceasing so that we develop an intimate relationship with God where we are in constant communication with Him. Sometimes we may need to find a good Christian counselor who will challenge our thinking. It may take reading spiritual books that are packed with the Word. Other times, we must seek the benefit of Christian programming on television (or radio) where ministers who are skilled at "rightly dividing the word of truth" (II Timothy 2:15) teach us how to apply the Word to our lives. We must use everything at our disposal if we want to be free.

The main thing that is important in breaking down a stronghold is to never give up. Purpose in your heart that you will have everything the Word of God says is yours by faith, no matter how long it takes. Refuse to settle for anything less and remember that, through the power of the Holy Spirit, you always triumph in Christ Jesus our Lord

OASIS FOR MY SOUL

(II Corinthians 2:14), you are victorious, and Satan is already defeated.


## REFLECTION

1. Do you currently have any strongholds in your life that you can identify? Write them down.

2. Search the scriptures to find out what God's Word says about the issues you identified above. Write out those scriptures.

3. Write down one confession regarding a stronghold in your life that you want to see torn down. Make sure it is in a positive format and includes scripture (e.g., "I am healed in my body by the stripes of Jesus" instead of "I am not sick in my body"). Confess it daily.

## PRAYER

Lord, I desire to be the best Christian I can be. I want to be whole and healthy in my emotions. Please help me identify any strongholds in my mind and give me a strategy for dealing with them. Thank You that, as I follow Your lead, Your Holy Spirit will guide me into all truth so that I can glorify You with my life. Thank You for the sanctification process that You are continuing within me today. In Jesus' name I pray, amen.

# CHAPTER THREE

## DAILY LIVING

This chapter contains poems dealing with topics that are necessary for spiritual maturity. These include spiritual lessons that God has presented to me over the years, some of which I am still trying to master. The entries will challenge you to grow spiritually, and they are designed to make you think twice about situations you may encounter in everyday life.

Trust and fear have an inversely proportional relationship. The more you trust God, the less you fear, and the more you fear, the less you trust God.

## *NO FEAR*

Satan has set a trap for believers,
For he is a liar and a master deceiver.
That trap called fear, designed to paralyze,
Is only a lie wrapped up in disguise.
You must feel the fear, but move out in God,
Go where no other man has trod.
That's the way to escape Satan's snare.
Do what you fear, and cast your care.
For God did not give you a fearful spirit,
The voice of Satan, refuse to hear it.
To live free of fear is a challenging task,
God will give you boldness if you'll only ask.
Declare God's Word as you attack your fear,
Ignore the devil's taunts and jeers.
Your fears you must identify,
Do not allow life to pass you by
Or let fear keep you in a little box
That Satan turns the key to lock.
Fear is designed to keep you still,
Know that, for you, that's not God's will.
Decide that fear will not control you,
Whatever the Father says, you must do.
Chase, capture, and wrestle fear to the ground,
Every single stronghold, bring it down.
Your heavenly Father will deliver, it's true,
When God gets done, Fear will fear you.

> "I sought the Lord, and he heard me,
> and delivered me from all my fears."
> **Psalm 34:4**

I read a book entitled *A More Excellent Way: A Teaching on the Spiritual Roots of Disease* in which the author, Pastor Henry Wright, purported that allergies are a result of fear.[5] I just happen to have a lot of allergies and chemical sensitivities, but I blew off his assertion. I said to myself, "I have no fear. This is nonsense." However, in the coming days, God "introduced me to myself." He reminded me of a time when I sat at a traffic light, and He told me to witness to someone I did not know in the car beside me, and I refused; that was because of fear. He showed me that I had a low-grade anxiety that followed me wherever I went. That was fear. He showed me that I was fearful of running out of money when I didn't have a job, even though He told me in His Word He would meet my needs. Fear. I couldn't identify these fears because I had lived with them for so long, they felt normal. God had put His finger on and identified the blind spots that I did not realize I had. Thank You, Lord.

God tells us in Psalm 34:4, we can live free of all fears. You may have read that and said to yourself, "That's impossible. We all have fear of some kind." I am not talking about fear of God. That type of fear involves reverence and honor of our Lord. I am not talking about healthy fear, such as the type of fear that will cause us to get away from real danger and take flight. I am not talking about the apprehension we all get when we step out and do something new. I am talking about fears that are unhealthy fears, such as phobias that control our lives, fears that keep us from doing what God told us to do, and perceived fears that cause us stress and anxiety although we really aren't in any danger. We can live free of all unhealthy fears if we trust God and ask Him to deliver us. As Jesus said in Matthew 9:29, "… According to your faith be it unto you."

God has given us spiritual weapons to completely defeat fear (II Corinthians 10:4). We simply have to take inventory of what God has given us and use those weapons to their maximum capacity. II Timothy 1:7 reads, "For God hath not given us the spirit of fear; but of power, and of love, and of a sound mind." Therefore, what He has given us to counteract the fear is the power of the Holy Ghost, the perfect love of God that casts out all fear (I John 4:18), and a sound mind, which is effectively the mind of Jesus Christ (I Corinthians 2:16). If we believe that the Power of the Holy Spirit supersedes the power of the devil, we will realize we have nothing to fear. If we believe that God loves us perfectly, then we will know that He is for us and fiercely protective of His own, and therefore the power of the Spirit will be dispatched on our behalf to rescue us from any adverse situation. When we activate the mind of Christ by studying the Word and gaining God's perspective, fear will leave.

In his book, *Fear Fighters*, Jentezen Franklin writes, "Either you give into fear and allow it to destroy your peace and well-being, or you become a warrior against it."[6] Therefore, when fear attacks us, we have to attack it. Here are some ways to do that:

1) Pray and ask God to deliver you from every one of your fears. (Psalm 34:4)

2) Scour the Word for scriptures about fear, and meditate on and declare them every chance you get. Make a special effort to speak out the Word when you are in fearful, anxiety-provoking situations. (Joshua 1:8)

3) Read every book you can about fear. Some good books I have read on the subject include: *Uprooting the Spirit of Fear* by Dr. Creflo A. Dollar; *Do It! Afraid* by Joyce Meyer; *30 Days to Taming Your Fears* by Deborah Smith Pegues; and *Feel the Fear and Do It Anyway* by Dr. Susan Jeffers.

4) Try writing fearful thoughts down in a journal and write out scriptures that counter the intrusive "thought bombs."

5) Continuously declare out loud your victory over your fears. (Job 22:28)

6) Purpose in your heart to do the very things you fear.

If you take these actions, you will put fear in its proper place in your life: under your feet.

To sum it up, Debra Smith Pegues said it best while promoting her book, *30 Days to Taming Your Fears*, on the *Today with Marilyn and Sarah* (Marilyn Hickey Ministries) television broadcast. She profoundly said that if we want to overcome our fear, we should follow the example set for us in I Samuel 17:48 and "run toward the fear as David did with Goliath—declaring God's Word all the way."[7] Thus, when you couple the Word of God with bold action steps, fear does not stand a chance. Take action to destroy any fear in your life that tries to stand between you and your destiny, and Fear will fear you.

# REFLECTION

1. What fears do you have in your life right now that are holding you bound? Ask God to help you to identify those fears.

2. What scriptures can you find to address those fears? Write them down and commit them to memory.

3. What action do you need to take to do the thing that you fear? Purpose in your heart to take a step of faith as you declare God's Word and "do it afraid."[8]

# PRAYER

Dear God, I thank You that You did not give me a spirit of fear (II Timothy 1:7), but have given me everything that I need to overcome fear in my life. Please help me coordinate my efforts and tap into the power of Your Spirit to stamp out the fears that bind me. As I study Your Word and take steps of faith, doing that which I fear, I thank You and believe that You will deliver me from all the unhealthy fears that I have been tolerating until now. In Jesus' name I pray, amen.

## WHAT IS FINANCIAL SECURITY?

What is financial security?
Is it owning bonds and stocks?
God is our only security,
And He surely will not be mocked.
Stock prices may take a tumble,
Every bank in the nation may fold,
But heaven will never be bankrupt
With pearled gates and streets of gold.
When the Wall Street gang did their dirty deeds
And the economy melted down,
God was not sitting up in Heaven
With a furrow in His brow.
He was not asking the Holy Spirit
And Jesus, "What shall We do?"
He knew all about it before it hit,
And man had no earthly clue.
The economy took a downward spiral,
The jobs then disappeared,
"Recession" became that dirty "R" word
That made grown men shed a tear.
The Dow Jones Industrial Index
Continues to rock and roll.
There's no need for a Christian to even blink
For God is so in control.
Before the recession came on the scene,
His plan was already formed
To keep you in the eye of the hurricane,
And to shelter you from the storm.
You may have lost employment,
Face foreclosure on your home,
But God is bigger than all of that,
He always takes care of His own.

*He promises to meet your every need,*
*Look to Him as your only Source.*
*You can count on Him to do what He says,*
*The Word of God is a formidable force.*
*When you are a part of the Kingdom,*
*You're in a different economy.*
*For the rest of the world it is not so,*
*For them what will be, will be.*
*But God has promised to provide for you,*
*To make it all work for your good.*
*There's simply no need to worry or fear*
*If you trust in your God as you should.*
*For true financial security*
*Is found in Jesus alone.*
*Look to Him, and your need He will supply,*
*God Almighty is still on His throne.*

> "Charge them that are rich in this world,
> that they be not highminded, nor trust in
> uncertain riches, but in the living God,
> who giveth us richly all things to enjoy."
> I Timothy 6:17

The way the economy has plummeted over the past few years has put fear in the hearts of many people. Jobs have been taken away. It's been said that 401(k)s have become "201(k)s." How can we maintain our peace and stability in the midst of such financial turmoil? The only way we can do it is to recognize that true financial security is found in God alone.

Consider the parable that Jesus told about the man in Luke 12:16-21 who was so filthy rich he didn't have enough space in the barn to store his goods. He decided he would tear down the old barn and build a bigger barn, store all of his "fruits" and "goods," and take it easy and enjoy life. But the scriptures go on to say in verse 20 that God told him, "Thou fool, this night thy soul shall be required of thee: then whose shall those things be, which thou has provided?" God is saying that anyone who trusts in his or her own ability to provide for themselves is a "fool." (I didn't say it, God did.)

When I was forced out of my job for health reasons, by the grace of God I had ample emergency savings. But I began to ponder, "Suppose my business ventures don't pan out? What if things take longer than I expect and the money runs out?" Then worry began to set in. The devil injected doubt into my mind, and I began to become fearful that my situation would not work out. I was so focused on what I could do, how much savings I had, and how quickly it was dwindling that I forgot to factor God into the equation. That is why I lost my peace. I failed to remember that God was my source, not my bank account, and not a job. When I "came to myself," I realized I had forgotten that God had never failed me, and when I needed a job, I always got one right on time. But that's what happens when we "trust in uncertain riches." That's what happens when we are so "high-minded" that we start to think we are making our own way, thinking that we are providing for ourselves, and have a sense of self-sufficiency.

God is not pleased when we become self-sufficient. Self-sufficiency is spelled "P-R-I-D-E." Again, the only financial security that we truly have is in our Lord and Savior, Jesus Christ. Our financial security is tied up in our eternal security, and our God is faithful to His Word. He will always do exactly what He says He will do. Thus, when the Creator of the Universe relays in Psalm 34:10, "… [T]hey that seek the Lord shall not want any good thing," He means just that. Now *that's* true financial security.

## REFLECTION

1. Think about a time when you faced a financial difficulty. What thoughts came to your mind? What emotions did you experience?

2. Think about a time when you had plenty of resources to meet your needs. What thoughts came to your mind? What emotions did you experience?

3. If worry, doubt, and fear have somehow worked their way into your psyche regarding your finances, how will you respond to counteract them?

4. Ponder the situations that you cited in the previous questions, then take into account what you've read in the above passage. What will you do differently in the future?

## PRAYER

Dear God, thank You for providing for my every need. Thank You for being faithful to Your Word and never letting me down. You have a superb track record and deserve my trust. Help me believe You and trust You even when my physical senses send me messages that are contrary to Your Word. Help me know that I can depend on You no matter what economic circumstances are going on around me. In Jesus' name I pray, amen.

# THE MAGIC EYES

Lord, give me Magic Eyes to see
All the good you do for me.
It's easy to see what's not going right
And ignore the things that are in clear sight.
For all the positive things You do,
Oh Lord, I should be thanking You.
For every coin does have two sides,
The same is true when troubles arise,
Whenever there is unpleasantness,
There is also evidence that I've been blessed.

If I had the Magic Eyes to see,
Then I would see things differently.
Your protective hand has held back disaster,
My negative thoughts I have to master.
My outlook must change; I know it's true,
I need to express gratitude to You.

The negative seems so big in my mind,
But if I look really hard, I'll always find
That the good far outweighs the bad,
Yet I take that for granted, and that's very sad.
I need those Magic Eyes, Dear Lord,
So that I can be obedient to Your Word.
I must find something to be thankful for,
I won't complain and open a door
For discouragement to come and weigh me down,
That's the trick of Satan, I know that now.

*I have to recognize the good,*
*So that I can praise you as I should.*
*I've got to notice what's NOT happening,*
*And be able to focus on the positive things.*
*Lord, please give me the Magic Eyes*
*To shrink the negative down to size,*
*So I can see all of Your goodness;*
*Only then will I see that I'm truly blessed.*

**"In everything give thanks: for this is the will
of God in Christ Jesus concerning you."
I Thessalonians 5:18**

Gratitude is a powerful thing. We need to thank God whenever we get the chance. Paul says in Philippians 4:6, "Be careful for nothing; but in every thing by prayer and supplication with thanksgiving let your requests be made known unto God." Therefore, prayer should always be coupled with thanksgiving. In I Thessalonians 5:17-18, we are told to pray without ceasing and give thanks. Therefore, to a Christian, thankfulness should be like breathing.

Why does God want us to look for things to be thankful for? One reason is because thankfulness shrinks our problems down to size. When we deliberately look for how the circumstance is working for our good, like Romans 8:28 says, then the negative aspects of our lives seem to fade into the background. We must always look for ways in which the thing that is causing us grief is working to our advantage. We know that it is working to our advantage because God says it is.

In the book of James, this same concept is relayed in a different way. In James 1:2 we read that we should count it all joy when we have trials of various kinds because they are working something good in us, namely patience. God wants us to get this: No matter what our physical senses tell us, things that seem bad to us are always working to our advantage. The question is, do we believe that? If we believe that, then come what may, we will have a thankful heart.

The problem is that the negative things seem to scream at us. Just like when we cut our finger or stub our toe, the rest of our body can be pain-free, but that finger or toe really smarts. Negative things are usually those that cause us pain of some kind. However, we must develop the practice of distracting ourselves with thanksgiving and praise for the many things that are going right in our lives. At first it will take conscious effort on our part. But after a while, the practice will become automatic, and we will be able to quickly divert our attention to the advantage the situation affords us and experience joy.

For example, I recently had a virus on my computer that pretty much shut me down as far as getting things done on my "to do" list. You know how it is. We've come to depend on computers and the Internet so much, that when we don't have access to them, it's like we're dead in the water. The company I hired to remove it did not do their job, so I had to get another company to finish the job. During that time, I was very frustrated, and lost my peace. Not once did I think about how the situation might be working to my advantage. After the ordeal was over and I got my computer up and running, I was able to see the lessons I could take away from it. A good thing that happened is that since I could not use my computer, I was able to get some things done that had been on my list forever. God made the decision about when I was to do those things. Once I got on the other side of the computer ordeal, I found that I did not lose any files (another thing to be thankful for). I got a chance to use what I had learned about decreeing something and watching it be established (Job 22:28). I kept saying aloud, "My computer will be restored." I tried to avoid complaining about what was or was not happening. God saw me through the situation, but unfortunately my peace waned, so I still have some growing to do. I should have asked myself, "What is God trying to do here? How can this thing work to my advantage?" Perhaps I would have stayed more peaceful on the inside.

How we look at a situation determines our response to it. If we choose to look for the positive, our response will be gratitude. If we look for the negative, our response will be complaining and negativity. Jerry Minchinton, author of *Maximum Self-Esteem: The Handbook for Reclaiming Your Sense of Self-Worth,* writes, "Since the option of selecting a positive perspective is always open, why should we subject ourselves to the pain and discomfort of a negative one?"[9] So, from this point forward, let's purpose in our hearts to look for the positive aspects in every negative situation. Let's look for ways that God can use the irritations in our lives to our advantage.

## REFLECTION

1. Do you currently have a difficult situation that you are walking through? Write it down.

2. What positive things can you glean from the situation you are facing? What might God be trying to accomplish in you through your trial? What are some possible positive results?

3. Write a praise statement to God about some aspect of the situation. "Lord, I praise You for ...."

## PRAYER

Dear God, I am so grateful that You are omnipotent and You know what is best for me. I appreciate the fact that You are so powerful that whatever happens in my life, You are able to turn it around and make it work for my good. Please help me train my mind to immediately look for how any circumstance that I find myself in may benefit me, and let me become good at finding things to thank You for. Thank You in advance. In Jesus' name I pray, amen.

## THE BOOMERANG OF JUDGMENT

*The Bible tells us not to judge,*
*But we all have had our shot*
*At judging others and implying to them,*
*We're perfect, and they're not.*
*We constantly judge what others do,*
*Of ourselves we have lofty views.*
*If it were not for the pure grace of God*
*We'd be doing the same things, too.*
*If God tells us that we should not judge,*
*Then judgment's a blatant sin.*
*When we judge the actions of those around us,*
*We know that we have pride within.*
*Who are we to judge the Lord's servant?*
*They don't answer to us anyway.*
*For we all answer only to God up above,*
*To Him only all homage we pay.*
*God is able to make His servant stand,*
*In spite of us, He will choose to bless.*
*He'll accept him although he's not perfect,*
*For He's clothed him in His righteousness.*
*Yet we habitually look down on others*
*With a superior, unkind attitude,*
*God is not pleased with those who think,*
*"You're less than; I'm better than you."*
*If we can do something better than they,*
*It's merely because of God's grace.*
*There's absolutely nothing to boast about,*
*It's humility we need to embrace.*

When we see that others are struggling with sin
We've the nerve to say, "How could they?"
We may have the victory in our lives right now,
But we'd better thank God and pray.
For we don't know the whole story,
And we never know what we would do
If we had walked a mile in their shoes
And been through what they had been through.
For God wants us to be like Him,
Love and mercy He always shows,
For if we show mercy, the Word is clear,
We always will reap what we sow.
But if we should choose to sow judgment,
We can be very sure that we'll find
That judgment is just like a boomerang
That will come back to us every time.
It's really a massive stronghold
That will often refuse to budge
Until we realize it, seek God, and pray,
"Dear Lord, help us not to judge."

"Do not judge, or you too will be judged.
For in the same way you judge others,
you will be judged, and with the measure
you use, it will be measured to you."
Matthew 7:1-2 (NIV)

The devil tempts us to judge people all the time. We are constantly presented with information that we could form an opinion about and then take an attitude of superiority. "I'd never do that!" we say to ourselves. When that happens, we have taken Satan's bait, and he has basically caught us in his snare. When we judge others (i.e., look down on them because they are different from us in some way), we have effectively committed a sin. Anything that God tells us not to do, and we do it anyway, is called S-I-N. Ouch.

Thus, whenever I hear information about someone, I have a choice to make: Will I take a superior attitude, forgetting that the only reason I am not in the same predicament as those I would judge is because of the grace of God? Or will I listen, suspend judgment, thank God for His grace, and take time to pray a silent prayer, asking Him to help my brother or sister in whatever way is needed?

I remember when the Lord started dealing with me on this issue. I was in a counselor's office, and she told me, point blank, that I was judgmental. I really didn't want to hear it, but it was true. It was something I needed to work on. I needed the power of the Holy Spirit to intervene on my behalf to help me be merciful to people. I couldn't "white-knuckle it" and beat this thing on my own. It was too deeply ingrained. God was not pleased with my prideful, self-sufficient attitude, and I had to change.

First, I began to catch myself judging people. That was huge. Before, I hadn't even thought about it. God also dealt with me about judging myself for being judgmental! When I caught myself being judgmental, the Holy Spirit reminded me that I should not condemn myself, and that the Bible says in Romans 8:1, "Therefore, there is now no condemnation for those who are in Christ Jesus."

Next, God told me I needed to stop judging people and situations verbally. I felt conviction when I spoke judgmentally about people and situations. I needed to be swift to hear and slow to speak and simply keep my mouth shut. I had judgmental thoughts, but at least I didn't say anything. That was a major breakthrough.

The next goal the Spirit set for me was to get to the place where I was able to listen and replace the judgmental thoughts with the Word of God. According to Dr. Creflo Dollar, senior pastor at World Changers Church in College Park, Georgia, the best way to counteract renegade thoughts is to speak the Word out of my mouth. He states, "Speaking the Word is a powerful double-whammy to the devil. First, it stops the demonic thought in its tracks. Then it follows up by attacking that thought with the audible Word of God."[10] I had to find at least one scripture that I could speak out loud to keep judgmental thoughts at bay. My favorite scripture to quote in that moment of temptation is Matthew 7:1 (NIV). Jesus said, "Judge not, or you too will be judged."

Finally, I started to pray for individuals when I was tempted to judge them. Prayer will do so much more for people than judgment. I began to ask the Holy Spirit to enlighten them and give them the power to do what they couldn't do by themselves. I also have to pray for myself. I have to constantly ask God to keep me from falling into the sin of judging them by saying, "Lord, help me not to judge." Galatians 6:1 says, "Brethren, if a man be overtaken in a fault, ye which are spiritual, restore such an one in the spirit of meekness; considering thyself, lest thou also be tempted." I not only have to beware of falling into the same sin they have committed, but also the sin of judgment and having a superior attitude.

If you are a judgmental person, know that you're not alone. I still struggle with this on a daily basis. It's a habit that has been formed over time, and you will need the help of the Holy Spirit to get control of it. Maybe you grew up in a home where judgment was abundant and mercy was scarce, and judgment is simply a knee-jerk reaction. In order to become free of this stronghold (for that is exactly what it is), the first step is to admit to God that it is a problem, then repent and seek His help.

As believers, it's important for all of us to stay humble. Judging others is a pride issue, and it is the height of self-exaltation. I Peter 5:5 (NIV) says, "[C]lothe yourselves with humility toward one another, because, 'God opposes the proud, but gives grace to the humble.' Humble yourselves, therefore, under God's mighty hand, that He may lift you up in due time." This means that if we don't humble ourselves, we can be guaranteed that God will humble us. In fact, Proverbs 16:18 says that "Pride goeth before destruction, an haughty spirit before a fall."

Therefore, let's purpose in our hearts to conquer the temptation of judging others. In I Corinthians 10:13, we read, "There hath no temptation taken you but such as is common to man: but God is faithful, who will not suffer you to be tempted above that ye are able; but will with the temptation also make a way to escape, that ye may be able to bear it." The way of escape is recognition, repentance, reticence, repetition of scripture, and reverent prayer. The change will not come overnight, but as we seek the help of the Holy Spirit, we will gradually and habitually be able to bless others, suspend judgment, and pray for them instantly.

## REFLECTION

1. Can you think of a time recently when you had a judgmental attitude toward someone? What was the circumstance?

2. Looking back on the situation, how would Jesus want you to think about it? How would He want you to respond?

## PRAYER

Dear God, please help me not to be judgmental. I recognize that when I judge others, I am increasing the likelihood of being judged myself. I pray for humility and the ability to always realize that Your Spirit empowers me to do anything that is right and good. Help me remember to pray for those around me instead of judging them. In Jesus' name I pray, amen.

## NOTHING TO FORGIVE

*The devil will try to make us think*
*We are less than who we are,*
*He uses others to pierce our souls,*
*He's been relentless from the start.*
*From the time we emerged from our mother's womb*
*To this time in our lives right now,*
*He's used people that we've encountered*
*To offend us and bring us down.*
*If we're not filled with the Word of God,*
*We're vulnerable to deeds and words,*
*Criticism, remarks, and sarcasm,*
*Hurtful comments that we've heard.*
*For our worth and value is immutable,*
*Truth is settled forevermore,*
*The enemy's words cannot ever mar*
*The image of God at our core.*
*What happens to us simply cannot change*
*The course of our true destiny;*
*We must never allow ourselves to believe*
*We are less than God made us to be.*
*For He deposited treasure in us*
*Under maximum security,*
*It's locked away in a sacred vault*
*Kept away from the enemy.*
*We are sealed by His Holy Spirit,*
*Enveloped by His love and grace,*
*On the inside we can not be changed*
*No matter what trials we may face.*

*As long as we hold onto false beliefs*
*We'll fall prey to the devil's mess,*
*We'll surely be caught in his deadly trap,*
*The snare of unforgiveness.*
*But when we are steeped in the truth of God,*
*When we truly grasp reality,*
*When we see that it's all a smoke screen*
*Orchestrated by the enemy,*
*When we realize that no matter what he says*
*We can still be positive,*
*We'll say to ourselves, "They can't touch me.*
*There's nothing to forgive."*

"A man's wisdom gives him patience;
it is to his glory to overlook an offense."
Proverbs 19:11 (NIV)

One day, I was talking on the phone to a friend of mine, and in the course of the conversation, my friend said something to me that was hurtful. When that happens, my way of dealing with it is to first write in my journal to see if I can resolve the issue within myself. If I cannot, then it's time to lovingly confront that person.

When I sat down, got quiet and examined the incident, I realized what the problem was. I had inadvertently forgotten something that was important to my friend, which made the person feel offended and possibly insignificant. So then the individual came back with an unnecessary comment to make me feel insignificant. It was a put-down and meant to hurt me. However, I have come to realize that when people are hurt, they often try to hurt others, thinking that will somehow help them alleviate their own emotional pain. So, when others hurt our feelings, a good place to begin the analysis is to trace the conversation back to see if there's a possibility that we have inadvertently hurt them in some way. When we come from a place of understanding, it is easier for us to overlook an offense.

My job at that point was to get over the hurt and forgive. In order to do that, the truth I needed to grasp at that moment was that no matter what people say to me, God has established my worth and value. He had declared it from the foundation of the world that I am fearfully and wonderfully made. When I accepted Christ as my Savior, I was declared fully righteous and nothing can ever change that. I am created in the image of Almighty God and my worth and value are grounded in that reality. The value that God has assigned to me is irrefutable and irreversible. All of us must ultimately grasp this truth if we are to stay sane in this world and be able to overlook offenses. When we realize this, it's as if God puts a force field around us, and when people strike out at us, we observe it but don't feel the impact of it.

Therefore, if the Word says that we are the righteousness of God in Christ once we have accepted Christ as our personal Savior (II Corinthians 5:21), what God has declared cannot be altered, and His Word will not return to Him void (Isaiah 55:11). Therefore, if we allow ourselves to let others alter our perception, we are virtually calling God a liar. He says in Luke 10:19, "Behold I give unto you power to tread on serpents and scorpions, and over all the power of the enemy: and nothing shall by any means hurt you." If He said that, it must be true. But the key to not being hurt is to know the truth that nothing, absolutely nothing, can change your worth and value, your destiny, the blessings God has for you, and the state of your righteousness before Almighty God. Once you lay hold to the truth, you will realize that when people lash out at you as a result of their internal pain, there is really nothing to forgive.

## REFLECTION

1. Can you think of a time when someone hurt your feelings? What happened and how did you deal with it?

2. In light of the new information that you have, what truth can you apply to that same situation?

## PRAYER

If necessary, please take time to pray right now and ask God to heal that wound and help you forgive the person and release the pain.

Dear God, please help me grasp the fact that I have infinite worth and value so that no one can convince me otherwise, regardless of what they do or say. Help me be slow to take offense and quick to forgive when necessary. Better yet, help me get to the point where I don't even need to forgive because the offense never gets into my heart in the first place. In Jesus' name I pray, amen.

# DIE EMPTY

I am determined to die empty,
Every gift, every talent God placed in me,
Will be used for His eternal glory;
I am destined to live victoriously.
I'll pour myself out like a drink offering,
I'll overcome any obstacle that Satan brings,
In my heart, sing a song of thanksgiving,
As I accomplish my goals, God's praises I'll sing.
The battle may be fierce and hot,
But I will not succumb to Satan's plot.
I will give it everything I've got,
Mediocrity will never be my lot.
My life will count, you wait and see,
I will not accept "what will be, will be."
Everything God put in will come out of me,
I'll live Spirit-filled, but I'll die empty.

"Having then gifts (faculties, talents,
qualities) that differ according to the
grace that is given to us, let us use them."
Romans 12:6 (AMP)

God has deposited gifts and talents into all of us, and we must be determined to use them all for His glory. To not use the positive attributes He gave us is unconscionable. Many people fail to use their treasure because doing so requires risk-taking and serious effort. We must risk failure and the possibility of embarrassment. Therefore, if we are ever to reach our potential we must be determined to push past our fear and complacency and, at times, risk appearing inept before the world.

In his book, *Understanding Your Potential*, Myles Munroe has a lot to say about fulfilling our potential in Christ. He writes, "People who die without achieving their full potential rob their generation of their latent ability.... To die with ability is irresponsible.... Release your ability before you die."[11] Thus, as Christians, we must seek God earnestly to determine what gifts and talents we have that we can use for the Kingdom—and use them to the best of our ability.

Paul was one of those people who gave his all for the cause of Christ. He relays to Timothy in II Timothy 4:6-7 (NIV), "For I am already being poured out like a drink offering, and the time has come for my departure. I have fought the good fight, I have finished the race, I have kept the faith." The term "being poured out" indicates that Paul was in the process of emptying himself of all the good treasures that God had deposited in him. He was coming to the end of his life, had no regrets, and was confident that he had given God his best. We all should follow his sterling example.

We need to know what our gifts are, and then figure out how to leverage them for the Kingdom. I feel that God has gifted me with creativity. I have many ideas, but now the challenge is to implement them. I am depending on God to give me a step-by-step plan to bring these dreams and visions to pass to benefit the Kingdom. This book is the first of the dreams that I am pursuing, and at the end of my life, I am determined to not have any regrets. I don't want to have to sit back in my old age and think, "I wonder what would have happened if...." Do you?

What ideas do you have that have been marinating in your spirit? What are the dreams that you have yet to pursue? You need to make a pact with yourself that you will pursue every dream and vision that God has put in your heart. Don't give any thought to the possibility of failure. As the old saying goes, "the road to success is paved with failure." All God asks you to do is to give Him your best, and He will be responsible for making it work. Promise yourself that you will pour out everything God has poured into you, and in the end, when you transition into the heavenly realm, you will hear Him say, "Well done, thou good and faithful servant" (Matthew 25:21).

## REFLECTION

1. What dreams and visions has God put in your heart that you have not yet pursued?

2. What would be the first step to accomplishing one of those dreams?

3. Who would benefit, and how, if you did accomplish what you set out to do?

4. Close your eyes and imagine yourself realizing your dream. Describe how you feel.

## PRAYER

Dear God, I want to accomplish Your perfect will for my life. Please help me identify any gifts and talents that lie dormant in me. Help me stay connected to You so that I can receive the power that I need to accomplish all that You have called me to do. I want to hear You say, "Well done." Therefore, I will do my best to make sure that I empty myself of all the gifts, talents, and treasures that You so lovingly and deliberately deposited in me. Let me be a gift to the body of Christ, well able to receive and appreciate the gifts You have placed in others as they pour themselves out for Your glory. In Jesus' name I pray, amen.

Feeling a little overwhelmed? That's a sure sign that you are trying to handle the situation totally by yourself. Now is the time to factor God into the equation.

# CHAPTER FOUR

## ENCOURAGEMENT

This chapter includes poems that will encourage you when you find yourself in the midst of tests or trials. This segment is packed with positivity and will help you hang in there when you are tempted to give up the fight. The entries will encourage you to trust God more than ever and believe Him for the miraculous.

## *WHEN GOD GIVES YOU A DREAM*

*When God gives you a dream in your heart*
*It's like you're pregnant with child,*
*You have all the signs that you're pregnant,*
*But you can't see that you are for a while.*
*When you can see yourself walking in*
*What God Almighty has planned for you,*
*If by faith you can see it and*
*In your heart it comes into view,*
*It's like looking at the ultrasound*
*Of the baby that leaps within.*
*The womb of your heart is carrying*
*A dream God Himself did send.*

*You watch your pregnant belly grow,*
*Your life is no longer the norm.*
*You even feel your baby kick*
*As your dream begins to take form.*
*At some point you go through transition,*
*Then the labor pains do start.*
*Sometimes things get so rough and painful,*
*Your journey seems so very hard.*
*For when you feel those birth pains*
*And those contractions come steadily,*
*You cannot abort the baby now,*
*For dilation has come so readily.*
*You must keep pushing, bearing down*
*No matter how painful it is,*
*You're birthing something into this realm,*
*A blessing that's so positive.*

*You cannot allow yourself to turn back*
*No matter how bad it gets,*
*You must keep pushing forward*
*Set your focus, and keep it set.*
*The babe now moves through the birth canal,*
*You simply cannot give up.*
*For God has given you the strength to hang on,*
*And keep your feet within the stirrups.*
*You feel the crown of the baby's head*
*As it emerges from your womb,*
*The baby that has been growing within*
*Will come into this world very soon.*

*Then finally your "child" is born,*
*That sweet little face you see,*
*The dream that God had put in your heart*
*Is now truly a reality.*
*You forget the pain of childbirth*
*And all that you went through,*
*When you finally have the dream in your hand*
*That God had promised you.*
*You see that it's all been worth it,*
*As painful as it may have seemed,*
*Remember that's how it happens*
*When God gives you a dream.*

"And it came to pass, that, when Elisabeth
heard the salutation of Mary, the babe
leaped in her womb; and Elisabeth
was filled with the Holy Ghost."
Luke 1:41

I was watching Dr. Creflo Dollar on the Trinity
Broadcasting Network (TBN) one day, and he made the
analogy between God giving you a dream that you can
envision coming to pass and a woman viewing her baby in
her womb via ultrasound.[12] When I heard that, it resonated
in my spirit, and I felt my "baby" leap within. I understood
exactly what He meant. We have to be able to see the
dream coming to pass by faith. Our "spiritual eyes" must be
able to see what God has purposed and planned for our
lives before it will ever be birthed into this earthly realm.

When God gives us a dream, it is always something
that is beyond our reach, something that we cannot pull off
by ourselves. If it is something that we can do alone, then
that's our own imagination. God is not going to give us
something that we can do and leave Him out. That just
promotes pride and self-sufficiency, which He wants to
avoid at all costs.

When you think about it, the way to stay close to God is
to always be striving to do something that you simply
cannot do by yourself. You have to put yourself in a position
where you feel you are in over your head at all times. That
means you must live on the edge and constantly listen to
the Spirit's direction to take risks. That is the way God
wants us to live, because then we will stay dependent on
Him. God wants us to be daring and believe Him for the

things that are "exceeding abundantly above" what any sane person would ask or think (Ephesians 3:20).

When you go for your dreams and live on the edge, two things happen: 1) You get to "see" God even though He is invisible. Through His supernatural maneuvers, He makes Himself tangible. 2) You stay close to Him because you have put yourself in a position to need Him desperately. In relationship with Him, there is a deep bond that develops out of your need for Him to help you to accomplish the dream He has put in your heart.

So don't be afraid to take risks. God loves it when you put yourself in a position that forces you to depend on Him. That pleases Him and deepens your fellowship with Him. When you live on the edge, that's when you really live. Let your dream cause you to live on the edge and watch God show out in your life.

## REFLECTION

1. Have you ever had a dream that looked like it would never come to pass? What will you do to make your dream live again? How can you go around the obstacles in your path?

2. Do you have a dream that you have not pursued because you are afraid to take a risk? What can you do to build your faith and overcome your fear so that you can step out and do what God has called you to do?

## PRAYER

Dear God, thank You for the dream that You have given me. Please empower me by Your Spirit to do my part, and I trust that You will do your part to make this happen. I want to be a blessing to Your people, and I know that is why You gave me this dream in my heart in the first place. Help me to not give up no matter what obstacles I encounter. I am determined that You will get glory out of my life. In Jesus' name I pray, amen.

## *SO YOU MADE A MISTAKE*

*OK, so you made a mistake.*
*OK, so you just "fleshed out."*
*Your best foot did not go forward,*
*But one thing you should never doubt:*
*Your Heavenly Father still loves you!*
*Just ask, He'll forgive your sin,*
*Tomorrow is a brand-new day,*
*And you can begin again.*
*He'll separate sin far from you,*
*He'll make your missteps work for good.*
*He'll give you the power to stand next time*
*And act like the Christian you should.*
*He is so awesome and gracious,*
*Full of compassion and mercy.*
*Those times when we slip and miss the mark*
*Are God's opportunity*
*To display His power and glory,*
*All our flaws and our weaknesses*
*Make us depend on Him more and more*
*As we strive to give Him our best.*
*Imperfections do keep us humble,*
*They just draw us close to His side,*
*So we don't become self-sufficient*
*And become too puffed up with pride.*
*So why not let yourself off the hook?*
*Why not give yourself a break?*
*For God has done so already,*
*Forgive yourself for Jesus' sake.*

**"As far as the east is from the west, so far hath he removed our transgressions from us."**
**Psalm 103:12**

We all make mistakes. We are human, and there is no escaping that. Sometimes when we make mistakes, we beat ourselves up and feel guilty for days. For the Christian, this should not be because we have accepted Jesus as our personal Savior, and when we fail, we are clothed in His righteousness. God sees us as righteous. He sees us as acceptable and OK. The question is: how do we see ourselves when we miss the mark? Even when we don't feel righteous, we have to act as if we are. Ask yourself, "If I had not done this or that, and I had acted as I should or could have, how would I feel or act?" Imagine that right now and bask in that feeling. Ahhhh. You would be walking with your head high and your shoulders back. You would feel as light as a feather. That feeling you have in your imagination is the way you should be feeling right now.

God wants us to see the world from His perspective, not our own. He does not want us to waste one minute in condemnation. When we wallow in condemnation after the Holy Spirit convicts us (for there is a difference between the two), our fellowship with God is hindered. Although nothing separates us from His love, during that time we feel as if we are separated from Him. We feel a sense of disconnection, and we lose our peace. This is certainly not the will of God.

We have to be able to repent, receive God's forgiveness, forgive ourselves (and others) as quickly as possible, and move on. Renowned poet, Maya Angelou, stated,

[W]hat I learned to do many years ago was to forgive myself. It is very important for every human being to forgive herself or himself because if you live, you will make mistakes—it is inevitable. But once you do and you see the mistake, then you forgive yourself and say, 'well, if I'd known better I'd have done better,' that's all.[13]

Thus, we can't help but make mistakes because it is impossible to know everything. Jerry Minchinton, author of *Maximum Self-Esteem*, states that "we do not make [mistakes] because we are stupid but because we lack information which would allow us to avoid them."[14] Given that, we really should foster an attitude of self-forgiveness.

Furthermore, why shouldn't we forgive ourselves if the Almighty God of the universe is willing to forgive us? Are we above Him? If He's accepted Jesus' sacrifice for our sins, why can't we? Holding a grudge against ourselves makes us feel disconnected from God, and that's when we are most vulnerable to the devil's attacks on our mind. We just can't allow that to happen. We must humbly admit our sin and believe I John 1:9, which says, "If we confess our sins, he is faithful and just to forgive us our sins, and to cleanse us from all unrighteousness."

When our humanity surfaces, we need to remember that God is so unlike us and the people around us. He is so compassionate and merciful that it may seem too good to be true. Although our weaknesses are innate, and we all have the sin principle operating in us, God is loving and patient when we fail. "For he knoweth our frame; he remembereth that we are dust" (Psalm 103:14). Thus, when we fail, that allows God to show us Who He really is, in all of His power and glory, as He extends His grace and mercy to us.

## REFLECTION

1. Think about the last time you had a hard time forgiving yourself. How long did it take you to confess it, repent, get over it, accept the forgiveness of God, and also forgive yourself?

2. If Jesus paid the penalty for your sin and you still feel guilty and condemned, you are trying to bear your own sin and pay your own penalty. If you have an area in your life where you have not forgiven yourself, what does Jesus' death on the cross mean to you in relation to that issue?

3. Jesus has paid the penalty for sins and mistakes past, present and future. Therefore, we don't have to allow the devil to hold us hostage in the prison of guilt and condemnation. Relive the scenario in your mind the way you think it should have happened, feel the feelings of that, then ponder this: That is the way God feels about you and wants you to feel about yourself even though things did not happen as you had desired. Jesus died to bestow a state of perpetual righteousness upon you, but you have to accept it and believe it in spite of your feelings. Are you ready to do that now? Ask the Holy Spirit to help you.

## PRAYER

Dear God, thank You for Your Son who died on the cross for my sins. Please give me a deep revelation of what it means to be righteous. Let me be able to accept the fact of my righteousness and let it penetrate my soul. Please heal me of the wound that causes me to dwell in condemnation when I fail. Let me be able to quickly and humbly accept Your forgiveness, Lord, and help me to forgive myself immediately, as well. In Jesus' name I pray, amen.

## GOD'S GOT YOUR BACK

*What you're facing may seem daunting,*
*It's challenging, that is true,*
*But nothing can thwart your destiny,*
*The plan God has for you.*
*The enemy may whisper,*
*"Oh, you will surely lack."*
*But surely he's a liar,*
*Know that God has got your back.*
*Fear and doubt may try to grip you,*
*But you've seen what God can do.*
*The Almighty One will never fail,*
*He'll move heaven and earth for you.*
*So whenever your back is against the wall,*
*And the devil is on the attack,*
*All you have to remember is*
*That God has got your back.*

> "...Fear not, nor be dismayed; tomorrow go out
> against them: for the LORD will be with you."
> II Chronicles 20:17

Throughout the Bible we read about how God has always communicated to His people, "I have your back," meaning He will be available to fight our battles for us when necessary. When it seems like we are outnumbered or overwhelmed, He will always show Himself to be the deciding factor in our victories. "God is...a very present help in trouble" (Psalm 46:1).

For example, in the twentieth chapter of II Chronicles, when King Jehoshaphat heard that a great army was coming to attack his kingdom, he was so afraid that he sought God's help to deal with the onslaught. He commanded everyone in Judah to fast and pray. The Lord answered them through the prophet Jahaziel, saying, "Be not afraid nor dismayed by reason of this great multitude; for the battle is not yours but God's.... [T]omorrow go out against them: for the LORD will be with you" (verses 15-17). In other words, God told them, "Don't worry. I've got your back." So they went out to battle singing and praising God, the Lord set ambushes against the attackers, and the armies that came against Judah were defeated.

Look at II Kings, chapter six. When the king of Syria sent an army to surround the city of Dothan where Elisha the prophet and his servant, Gahazi, were located, Gahazi panicked and basically yelled at his master, "What are we gonna do?!" Elisha told him to relax because the enemy was outnumbered. The prophet then prayed that his servant would also see what he saw. Subsequently, the eyes of Gahazi were opened, and in the spirit realm, he saw a mountain full of horses and chariots of fire that had been deployed by God to protect them. Although help was not visible to the naked eye, the Almighty still had the backs of His servants. We too must remember that even though we can't see God and what He is doing behind the scene, it does not mean that He is not in control of the situation and a very present help in the time of trouble (Psalm 46:1).

What's so good about God is that He has our back consistently. We may have good friends that we know that will help us out when we need it. They have proven themselves to be faithful, and we love and appreciate them. However, even the best friend that we may have is fallible. At some point, because they are human, they will let us down. We may always try to be the best friend that we possibly can be, but unfortunately, we are "dust" and we must admit that we have let others down. As hard as we try, we just can't be perfect. Jesus is the only friend we have that will back us up and never fail us. Therefore, it's so good to know that we have a God that we can depend on and will always have our back. In fact, II Chronicles 16:9 says, "For the eyes of the LORD run to and fro throughout the whole earth, to show himself strong in the behalf of them whose heart is perfect toward him." That means that God is constantly looking for ways to back us up.

When we are up against seemingly insurmountable odds, the natural response is fear and a feeling of being overwhelmed. However, if we remember that we never go into any battle alone, that God is with us to help us and make His supernatural power available to us, then we can rest in Him. Satan, our adversary, is no match for the God who is with us and within us. The Lord has promised He will not fail or forsake His children. So no matter what you are facing today, God has this message for you: "I've got your back." Therefore, go forth in confidence.

## REFLECTION

1. Can you think of ways in the past where you found it to be true that God had your back?

2. Are you facing anything in the future where you need God to have your back? What are your expectations of God in the situation and what scriptures can you find to support that expectation?

## PRAYER

Dear God, thank You for Your faithfulness to me. Thank You for always having my back. Please help me to remember that when I am facing seemingly impossible odds, I can always trust You to keep Your Word to me. Help me to realize in my heart that as long as You are with me and I trust You, I will never go under in defeat because You always cause me to triumph in Christ Jesus through the power of the Holy Spirit (II Corinthians 2:14). I praise Your Name because You are truly an awesome God who takes care of His children. Thank You for Your abiding presence. In Jesus' name I pray, amen.

## MY ROCK IS NOT ENOUGH

*David killed Goliath*
*With a rock and a slingshot,*
*In the natural that seems ridiculous,*
*But when God's involved, it's not.*
*The boy ran toward the battle line*
*With everything he had.*
*Goliath cursed him up and down,*
*The giant was armor clad.*
*David then swung his slingshot,*
*And a smooth stone, he let fly.*
*God guided that rock like a missile,*
*And Goliath was destined to die.*
*The huge Philistine was struck in the head*
*And knocked down to the ground.*
*God's anointing made the difference,*
*And the victory brought David renown.*
*So his rock was simply not enough,*
*For the giant was too big and tall.*
*Only God's power could ever make*
*Goliath tumble and fall.*

*What do you do in a battle*
*When your rock is not enough?*
*You can't see how you'll ever win,*
*But you must call Satan's bluff.*
*He throws punches relentlessly,*
*He throws them left and right.*
*You want to turn and run away,*
*But you know you must stand and fight.*

*You fight with everything you have,*
*You make little or no progress.*
*You're truly doing the best you can,*
*Then you realize you must digress.*
*You finally admit to yourself and God,*
*"My rock is not enough."*
*You must admit you're overwhelmed,*
*This battle is just too rough.*

*When You've taken a serious beat down,*
*And the rock you have thrown has missed,*
*Let God get a hold of the next rock you have,*
*Let Him with His power assist.*
*You cannot win without God's help,*
*To get Satan's onslaughts to stop,*
*You must call on Jesus for backup*
*If you're ever to end up on top.*
*You must get a Rhema Word from God*
*That your rock is just not enough,*
*Your situation is bigger than you,*
*But your God is big, and He's tough.*
*You must tell yourself, "It is what it is,"*
*You're inadequate for this task,*
*And God is simply standing by,*
*He'll help if you'll only ask.*
*He'll help You to win the battle,*
*And you'll gain a sweet victory.*
*Just keep the faith, He'll carry you through,*
*For you, He'll part the Red Sea.*

So, you see, it does not matter
That your rock is not enough.
As long as God is by your side
Whenever the going gets tough.
The best thing you could ever do
Is to cast your care on God.
The battle certainly is not your own,
For Him nothing is too hard.
All you need to do is close your eyes,
Just sling your rock and pray,
And ask the Lord to hit the mark,
And victory is yours today.
He will take hold of that rock mid-air,
Carry it to its target, that's true.
Your giant will be brought down for sure,
God will surely fight for you.
Remember it's not your ability
That will bring you safely through,
But the power of God coupled with your best,
Only that combination will do.
So when the devil tries to tell you,
"Your rock is not enough,"
Just tell him, "You know what? You're right!"
And allow God to strut His stuff.

And David put his hand in his bag,
and took thence a stone, and slang it,
and smote the Philistine in his forehead,
that the stone sunk into his forehead;
and he fell upon his face to the earth.
I Samuel 17:49

My bishop, Dr. B. Courtney McBath, gave an excellent sermon entitled, "What Do You Do When Your Rock is Not Enough?" This was the inspiration for the poem you just read. Bishop preached from I Samuel 17, which gives an account of David's battle with the giant, Goliath, in the valley of Elah. In that passage, the shepherd boy constantly talked about what God did and what He would do. In verse 37 David says, "The LORD that delivered me out of the paw of the lion, and out of the paw of the bear, he will deliver me out of the hand of this Philistine." In verses 45-46 he tells Goliath, "Thou comest to me with a sword, and with a spear, and with a shield: but I come to thee in the name of the Lord of hosts, the God of the armies of Israel, whom thou hast defied. This day will the LORD deliver thee into mine hand...." He didn't go before Goliath talking about the five smooth stones he had in his bag. He knew wholeheartedly that his "rock was not enough." He totally depended on God, his "secret weapon," to make the difference.[15]

I remember a time when I felt that my "rock" was not enough. When I was at college attempting to complete my Industrial Engineering degree, I had to take a computer class called "Simulation." It seemed they wanted us to simulate the entire world with a computer program. I had dreaded that class all throughout my college career because

I knew I wasn't that computer savvy. Programming computers was not my gift, but I was pursuing an engineering degree (that's another story). After I went to the first class and found out what I was truly in for, it terrified me because I felt that I just didn't have what it took to get through that class. I ran back to my room, got down on my knees beside my bed, and fervently prayed to God, telling Him that if He didn't help me, there was no way that I was going to make it through. I implored Him to help me to pass the class because, if failed it, I could not graduate that semester.

In class we were told that we had to do a computer simulation project that we needed to work in groups of three to complete. The sign-up sheet was in the professor's office. The next day I went there, and as I looked at the sign-up sheet for the groups, I asked the Lord which group I should sign up for. I wrote my name down and left the office. We were given our assignment as a group; I met with the two individuals at the appointed time, and received my portion of the assignment to work on. I wrote code to the best of my ability and did all that I was assigned to do. My team members consisted of one man and one woman who were both good at programming, but the guy turned out to be an absolute computer "guru." When all was said and done, we were the only group in the class that received an "A." I am not saying that to brag at all, because I know that "my rock was not enough." There was no way I would have gotten an "A" in that class without the help of God.

So how do you handle the giants in your life? What do you do when your rock is not enough? The only way to successfully handle what you are facing when it is bigger than you are is to admit that you are totally inadequate for the task, do your best, and depend on God to make the difference with His power. If you follow that paradigm, you too will defeat every "Goliath" that comes your way.

## REFLECTION

1. What situation are you facing right now that makes you feel "your rock is not enough"?

2. What are your expectations of God in this situation? What is the outcome that you would like to see?

3. What scriptures can you find in the Word to support your expectation of what God can and will do? Write them down.

## PRAYER

Dear God, I praise You for being the greatest power in the universe. I am facing a very difficult situation right now, and I feel that "my rock is just not enough." I need Your assistance and Your power. Please help me unreservedly put my faith and trust in You to see me through this situation. I know You will not let me down, and You will not leave or forsake me. You are able to do exceeding abundantly above all that I ask or think (Ephesians 3:20). Therefore, I thank You in advance for the victory. In Jesus' name I pray, amen.

# *JOY*

Thank You, Lord, this is not my lot.
Thank You, God, this is not all You've got
For me in this life,
Stress on top of strife;
This thing is temporary,
Although not ordinary.
For in this life we will have tribulation,
Highs, lows, and trauma,
Times of jubilation.
But the joy will come in the morning
In spite of what it looks like now.
In this fight I may be down, but I'm not out.
I am coming out with the victory shout.
I see it, I see it, before me now,
The joy, the triumph; my knee will not bow
To Satan's ploy to steal my joy.
I may suffer now, but
Up ahead is my destiny;
Up ahead is my purpose;
Up ahead is my victory.
Broken off is the curse,
The spell is now broken,
I refuse to give the devil a token.
I refuse to pay homage to the evil one.
My praise and my glory I'll give to the Son.

*My joy is unspeakable and full of glory,*
*I have a testimony, I have a story*
*Of how He saved me,*
*He delivered me from despair and depression,*
*How He gave me joy, freed me from oppression.*
*The devil deceived me into thinking I was done;*
*That was a lie, my freedom was won*
*On the cross two thousand years ago.*
*Then I thought of that victory,*
*I thought of my future,*
*I thought of God's faithfulness, imagined my destiny;*
*The joy welled up, and I was OK again.*
*I look forward to the day when deliverance is here,*
*The joy of it now just brings me to tears.*
*I'm out, I'm free,*
*He's delivered me, and now I live, His face I see.*
*I know my place, victory I taste,*
*His joy is mine, and I will win my race. Selah.*

## "[W]eeping may endure for a night, but joy cometh in the morning."
### Psalm 30:5

Joy is a supernatural sustaining force in our lives. The Bible calls it "fruit" because it's sweet, succulent, and nourishing to the soul. Galatians 5:22 says, "[T]he fruit of the Spirit is ... JOY." Hard times are always followed by joy (Psalm 30:5). That is a promise from God. As my pastor, Bishop B. Courtney McBath, would say, "The night cannot last forever." No matter what is going on in your life right now, as surely as the sun comes up in the morning, joy is coming. According to the version of Webster's dictionary published in 1828, "Joy is the delight of the mind, from the consideration of the present or assured approaching possession of a good."[16]

Joy is based in optimism and hope for a better tomorrow. Whatever is happening now may not be joyful, but must be counted as such. Why? Because of the benefit that will be evident in the future. However, if we are short-sighted, the joy will not come. We must be able to see, as Jesus did, the joy that is set before us (Hebrews 12:2). That requires that we look into the future and see what God says is ours by faith. We must see that the momentary, light affliction we are experiencing is going to manifest a ton of glory (II Corinthians 4:17). Boy, is that tough when you're going through a storm. Tough, but not impossible.

Whenever we are under severe trial, we must intentionally cultivate joy the way we would cultivate a tender plant. That means we must do those things that will cause our joy to manifest and grow. We must keep the Word constantly coming into our ears and heart. We must eat, sleep and breathe the Word. We must get in the presence of God as often as we can, we must watch Christian TV, we must read good spiritual books. We must engage in praise and worship regularly to help us be aware of God's power that is available to us. If we are to have joy and spiritual victory, the Word should be going into our ear-gate and eye-gate constantly.

The point is that we must create a "spiritual cocoon" around ourselves. The Word, coupled with the presence of God, becomes a capsule—a hiding place, if you will—and we become like a "caterpillar" until the trial is over and we emerge as a beautiful butterfly. But during the trial, if we practice the presence of God, we will surely be able to experience the fruit of the Spirit called "joy." Joy is a byproduct of saturating the spirit with the Word and presence of Almighty God. After all, God did say that in His presence, there is fullness of joy (Psalm 16:11).

## REFLECTION

1. Reflect on a time in the past that was so difficult that your joy was stolen. Looking back on the situation, how would you have handled it differently, knowing what you know now?

2. What was the outcome? How did God intervene?

3. If you are currently going through a trial that is stealing your joy, what is your strategy or plan for creating a "spiritual cocoon" for yourself? (i.e., what spiritual goals will you set for yourself that will build

you up and cause you to be spiritually strengthened and nourished?)

4. What scriptures can you find that comfort you during this time? Write two of them down and commit them to memory.

## PRAYER

Dear God, I praise You in the midst of what I am going through right now. This trial that I am under at the moment is not pleasant, but painful, and I thank You that You are using this circumstance to prepare me for my destiny. Thank You for Your presence and the fruit of Your Spirit called "joy." Help me do the things necessary that will cause the joy You have deposited in me to manifest during this difficult time in my life. Let it sustain me and enable me to glorify You. In Jesus' name I pray, amen.

## CHAPTER FIVE

# GRIEF

These poems were written to provide comfort in times of pain, loss, and distress that we all inevitably encounter. I want you to be able to sense that God is with you in fiery trials and that He cares deeply about what you are experiencing. Hopefully, you will be reminded of Jesus' infinite power to heal us in our emotionally wounded state. Furthermore, I attempted to express through these poems what you may feel when you lose a loved one. My desire was to normalize the feelings that you may experience during the grieving process and, hopefully, get you to sense that someone, namely God, understands what you are going through. Most of all, I wanted you to feel the commonality of the grief experience for all of us.

The mature soul wholeheartedly depends on the living God. The ability to do so is the true measure of one's strength.

## I MISS YOU SO

I miss you so and wish you were here,
For there's no one now to calm my fears,
To wipe my tears, and tell me again,
"It will be OK, life's game you will win."
I miss you so.
I miss your smile.
I miss your spirit.
I miss your style.
I can't hold back, and I've got to be real.
My emotions are raw, and this is how I feel:
Life's not the same without the essence of YOU.
There's a void in my life,
I'm not sure what to do.
You left my world; I didn't want you to go,
And this is the truth I need you to know:
I miss you so.

## "I will not leave you comfortless:
## I will come to you."
## John 14:18

Nothing hurts like losing a loved one. If you had a wonderful relationship, it hurts because you will miss your beloved terribly. You will feel a void in your life because they added so much to your existence and brought you joy. If you had a turbulent relationship with them, it hurts because you grieve over the relationship that you never had and the one that never will be. Emotionally, you may feel like your heart is being ripped out of your chest. You may miss that person so much that your heart aches for them. That is the nature of grief.

If the person died in Christ, the good news is that we will see them again. But what do we do in the meantime? We can't just curl up and die and let the pain consume us. The pain may be unbearable; however, we have to go on. The question is, how? By taking a step day by day and drawing on the comfort of the Holy Spirit to see us through a very difficult situation.

In his book, *Good Grief,* Granger E. Westberg states that because we experience different types of grief on a small scale every day, "grief is as natural to every person as breathing."[17] He relays that when a loved one dies, we may go through ten different stages of grief. They can be experienced in any order, some stages may not be experienced at all, they may last varying lengths of time, and they can vary in intensity depending on the individual.

The first stage is shock, where God basically allows us to be "anesthetized" as a response to an overwhelming tragedy. Stage two is the expression of emotion. Stage three includes feelings of depression and loneliness. Stage four involves physical symptoms of distress. Stage five includes feelings of panic. In stage six we feel a sense of guilt about the loss. In stage seven, we may feel anger and resentment. Stage eight may involve resisting the return to our normal activities. In stage nine, we began to feel hopeful that we can carry on without our beloved. Finally, in stage ten, we come out of the experience different, for better or for worse, based on how we dealt with the situation at hand.[18] It's important to know what to expect so that we know that what we are experiencing is normal and that we are not going "crazy."

If you are mourning, know that God is truly a Comforter. In fact He says, "Blessed are those who mourn, for they shall be comforted" (Matthew 5:4). That is a promise. So, if you lost a spouse, the Bible says your Maker will be your spouse (Isaiah 54:5). If you lost a friend, the Word says, "[T]here is a friend that sticketh closer than a brother" (Proverbs 18:24). If it you lost a parent, David said in Psalm 27:10, "When [your] mother and [your] father forsake [you], the LORD will take [you] up." If you lose a child, He promises that He will not leave you comfortless and will comfort you as any loving Father would His own child (John 14:18). Know that after He comforts you and heals you, and the devastation of losing your beloved has passed, you will be able to comfort others who are hurting (II Corinthians 1:3-4). Though you may go through a very difficult trial, you will be able to take comfort in knowing that although the person you miss may have been removed from your life, their memory can never be stolen from your heart.

## REFLECTION

1. When you have a minor loss, how do you respond?

2. If you have ever experienced a major disappointment or loss, answer these questions:

   a. How did it negatively impact you?
   b. How did it impact you for the positive?
   c. What did you learn about yourself during that process?
   d. What did your loss teach you about God?
   e. How did what you learned change the way you respond to people who are mourning?

## PRAYER

Dear God, thank You for sending Your Holy Spirit, the Ultimate Comforter. Whether I have a loss that is big or small, I recognize my need for continual dependence on You. When I experience a loss, as I inevitably will, help me put it in perspective in light of Your Word and what You mean to me. Help me move through my grief in a healthy way. Let the light of Your presence heal me and bring me to a place of wholeness, strength, and peace as this momentary, light affliction works an eternal weight of glory on my behalf (II Corinthians 4:17). I look to You as my Source of strength and comfort, and I give You praise for Who You are and for Your ability to bring good out of something so painful. In Jesus' name I pray, amen.

## LEFT BEHIND

*Oh, God, please be with those of us*
*Who are left behind down here.*
*Let your Holy Spirit comfort us,*
*Lord, now, we need You near.*
*For we don't always understand*
*Why things happen the way they do.*
*But, God, You're still upon Your throne,*
*Oh, Lord, we trust in You.*
*Please do a work in us, Oh God,*
*Please heal our wounded souls,*
*While we wait to see our loved one*
*In Heaven on streets of gold.*
*We will see our beloved once again,*
*We know Jesus has paved the way.*
*We look forward to a warm embrace,*
*And we'll cherish that joyful day.*

## "And the Lord said unto Samuel, 'How long will you mourn for Saul?'" I Samuel 16:1

Death of a loved one can feel like a terrorist attack on our lives. On September 11, 2001, when the Twin Towers fell in New York City, we felt fear. We felt a loss of security. Some of us lost loved ones, and therefore we felt grief. On the news, we saw people walking around in a daze as if they were in shock. People were walking around in what looked like a war zone. Post-Traumatic Stress Disorder (PTSD) was rampant. All of these feelings—along with feelings of confusion and abandonment—can be present when we lose a loved one.

How do we deal with the aftermath when we are left behind? How do we deal with the pain and agony of our grief? The answer is: the best way we can—through the power of the Holy Spirit. We must seek the Almighty God to heal us. We also must realize that everyone grieves differently. It is so important for us to grieve our way. If we need to talk, we should talk. If we need to cry, we should cry. If we need to seek a counselor, then we should seek help. But whatever we do, we must depend on the Holy Spirit, the Comforter, to do what He does best: Heal us where we hurt the most.

The important thing we must remember if we are to survive the "terrorist attack" of death is to make sure God is at the center of our lives. If we don't, then we will give the enemy an open door to wreak havoc in our world and stunt our ability to grieve in a healthy way. Healing and recovery will be prolonged and much more difficult, and we will likely remain stuck in our grief, cut off from the very source of healing that we need.

A friend of mine once told me, "If one of my children died, I don't know what I would do. I just wouldn't make it." I replied, "Sure you would, because God is the center of your world and when He is the center, no matter what happens, your world will not collapse." There was a pause, and then she said, "I have to go and think about that one."

We have to be careful that we don't make an idol out of anyone in our lives. God says, "Thou shalt have no other gods before me" (Exodus 20:3). This includes spouses, children, parents, and friends. Authors William Backus and Marie Chapian relay this wisdom in their book, *Telling Yourself the Truth*. They write, "If you believe you cannot live without a certain person or that your entire existence depends on somebody else, you are setting yourself up to be hurt by that misbelief.... The untruth lies in the fact that nothing and nobody but God is crucial to anyone."[19] When we start to believe that there is no truth to this assertion, then we have created a "golden calf" in our lives.

When we have God in His proper place, we are able to feel our pain, mobilize, heal, and move forward when tragedy strikes. This does not mean that our loved one didn't hold a special place in our hearts, that we don't hurt for a time, or that we did not love them dearly. It simply means that we loved them, but we refuse to give the devil the opportunity to destroy us. When we have people as the center, we put ourselves in an extremely vulnerable position. We open the door for the enemy to annihilate us emotionally and spiritually, and keep us from fulfilling the call on our lives. His goal is to get us to the place where we cannot effectively function in life. That is why we must be careful to make sure that God is the center of our world. It seems we are never prepared for the death of the ones we love. But if we make God our hub, then we will be better prepared to be left behind, and continue on our journey with God.

The question is not whether we will be left behind (since most of us experience the loss of someone we love in our lifetime), but how will we be left behind? Will we be a shattered mess? Will our lives totally collapse because we determined that our loved one was the foundation of our lives? Will we be unable to function or move forward because we depended on the one we loved as our source? Or will we grieve, cry, then and move confidently forward, depending on God for strength and expecting Him to meet every emotional, spiritual, and physical need as he promised in His Word?

We who are left behind will be able to show the world that God is the firm foundation of our lives, and that even though we have lost someone very near and dear to our hearts, we will survive, and not only survive, but thrive. We will hold the memory of our beloved in our hearts, but if he or she is saved, we will be able to have them look down from above and see that we are grieving in a healthy way, drawing strength from our God, and carrying on in a way that would make them very proud. And that's exactly what they would have wanted, isn't it?

## REFLECTION

1. Think about the important people in your life, and be honest with yourself. If any one of them left, do you believe you could not make it? If so, who is that person?

2. If you answered yes to the question above, how do you think God feels about your relationship with that person?

3. How do you communicate to God that He is the center of your world? (e.g., behaviors, thoughts, words, etc.)

## PRAYER

Dear God, I thank You that my life does not depend on anyone but You. Please help me be mindful of putting You first in my life. Let me not have any idols that I allow to take Your place in my life. Thank You for the comfort of Your Holy Spirit, Who is able to see me through any tragedy. I give You praise and glory that all things are working together for my good (Romans 8:28). In Jesus' name I pray, amen.

## GOD KNOWS YOUR PAIN

*God feels the anguish within your soul,*
*He sees each tear you cry.*
*The journey you take is not yours alone,*
*Jesus is right by your side.*
*He understands like no one else,*
*He knows what you're going through.*
*God is so wise and omniscient,*
*He always knows just what to do.*
*He'll never leave or forsake you,*
*You'll come through this in Jesus' name.*
*As He was in the furnace with three Hebrew boys,*
*He'll be with you, too, in the flames.*
*Jesus will heal you where you hurt,*
*He knows the depth of your pain.*
*His healing balm He will apply,*
*And you'll never be the same.*

"When you pass through the waters I will
be with you; and when you pass through
the rivers, they will not sweep over you.
When you walk through the fire, You will not
be burned; the flames will not set you ablaze."
Isaiah 43:1-2 (NIV)

Have you ever been at a place in your life where you were in so much emotional pain that you felt you would never be whole again? Maybe your heart was broken, or you experienced a major loss of some kind. Whatever you were going through, it probably seemed as if no one could understand the depth of your pain. You felt there was a hole in your soul, and there was nothing any human being could do to alleviate the anguish you were experiencing deep in the recesses of your being.

My great-nephew died of SIDS at the age of four months, and that was a very painful experience for our family to walk through. The promise and potential of his little life was taken away in an instant. I will never understand what it's like to lose a child, but I'm sure his parents, my nephew and his wife, felt deep, gut-wrenching emotional pain that was relentless. They experienced heartbreak of tremendous proportions, and surely God felt every bit of their agony. After all, His son also died prematurely.

Thankfully, when we lose a loved one, the Holy Spirit knows exactly how we feel, He understands us as individuals and is able to comfort us in our grief. He is in the furnace of life with us, and His omniscience allows Him to truly understand our pain in a way that no one else can. Thus, we can draw comfort from the simple fact that

Someone understands. Additionally, when we hurt, God sends angels in the form of friends and loved ones who come alongside us and provide comfort through their presence, words, and acts of kindness that ease our pain and make our day a little bit brighter.

Through the comfort we receive, God desires to teach us how to comfort others so that He can move through us in a way that makes Him tangible, and this allows those who are hurting to feel His presence (II Corinthians 1:3-4). As Christians, we need to be able to comfort others and be a blessing to them when they are hurting. However, this will require us to take note of what people do for us in our time of sorrow that is comforting, and then, in turn, extend that graciousness to others. Conversely, we should also note those things that others do and say that are hurtful to us, so that we can avoid inflicting more emotional pain on people who are already hurting. We can learn lessons in the midst of our pain that will help us become agents of comfort. When we are able to comfort the hurting, we can be used by God to help facilitate their healing process. There is an old saying that "time heals all wounds," but only God can heal a broken heart. It is the Lord who heals our emotional wounds.

When trials and tests pierce your soul, you can rest assured that even though the pain may be unbearable at the moment, God is able to "stop the bleeding" and ultimately restore your emotional stability. He is able to provide the emotional first aid that you need when you continually bask in His presence and seek His face. That is the only way out of the pain.

In summary, when the death angel rears his ugly head, one thing we can be sure of is that our Father will never leave us or forsake us; He will stay close by our side in troubled times, make His presence known in spite of His spiritual invisibility, and bring us to a point of wholeness and spiritual maturity. We will never be the same after the experience, but we'll be better if we defer to His omniscience and simply allow Him to be God.

## REFLECTION

1. When you are going through troubled times, what can people do for you that makes you feel comforted? If you have not done so, why not take time to communicate this to your loved ones?

2. What have you done for others in their time of grief that they said made them feel comforted?

3. Can you remember a time when you (or someone you know) were grieving and someone said or did something that was not helpful, but hurtful? What happened, and what did it teach you?

## PRAYER

Dear God, thank You for how You have comforted and healed me emotionally. I praise You for Your understanding heart and for always loving me right where I am in the moment. You always fully understand what I am going through, and that is one of the things I love about You. I desire to be an agent of Your comfort. Help me be sensitive to the needs of others who are hurting. Please give me a Word in season to say to them that will be helpful and will allow me to represent Your presence accurately. Help me keep a gate over my lips so that I will not cause those who are hurting more pain. In Jesus' name I pray, amen.

## GOD IS YOUR HEALER

As a seed is planted into the earth,
And we know not the mystery of its birth
Into the plant God created it to be,
Your growth and deliverance you will see.
You bask in the light of Jesus, the Son,
Your journey toward wholeness has begun.
The Almighty works to remove the pain,
His divine power He sends like rain,
In His time, God will heal your soul,
Know that He'll indeed make you whole.
And though your progress seems very slow,
There is one truth He wants you to know:
You will be made anew.

"Therefore, if any man be in Christ, he
is a new creature: old things are passed
away; behold, all things are become new."
II Corinthians 5:17

All of us have areas in our emotions that need healing. None of us has it all together. We are yet being changed from glory to glory. When we came to Christ, we made a quality decision that we needed Jesus to help us because we came to the conclusion that we could not help ourselves. Thus, when we accepted Jesus as our personal Savior, the healing journey began.

When we became born again, the Spirit began to introduce us to ourselves and show us spiritual and emotional issues that needed to be addressed. As we read the "mirror" of the Word, we began to see character flaws that weren't pretty. As the Holy Spirit moved mightily in our lives, our imperfections were revealed to us for the purpose of conviction, which is "the act of convincing a person of error or of compelling the admission of a truth."[20] This is not to be confused with condemnation, which is the act of declaring something "to be reprehensible, wrong or evil."[21] Nevertheless, we still didn't always want to face what we saw, so we ran. Some of us are still running. We continue to keep busy and make a conscious choice to "keep it moving" so we will not have to look within. That is not the path that leads to healing.

Frankly, the true path that leads to healing involves time alone with God. There is no other way around it. I implore you, if you are one of those people who is constantly running to church every time the doors open, attending every social event that you can find, saying "yes" to every social invitation, and working yourself into "bone weariness" in an effort to avoid being home alone, please, STOP IT. The only way for God to get a Word to you is for you to be still and know that He is God (Psalm 46:10). The Holy Ghost cannot minister to a vessel that is constantly on the move. You must face the pain of being alone, if this is an issue for you. That is the first step.

Once the Holy Spirit shows us who we are and what needs to be changed about us, we usually want it to happen right away. Most of the time (and there are exceptions, because the Spirit can move as He wills), personal growth and inner healing is a gradual process that takes time. There are incremental changes. Sometimes our growth seems so slow that we barely feel like we are making any progress at all. The truth is that we are making progress no matter how "stalled out" we may feel. The important thing is that we must keep doing everything the Spirit instructs us to do.

I'll never forget when I first realized I needed to make some changes in my life. I became painfully aware of the personal growth that needed to take place within my soul. On July 2, 1982, I drew up a contract with myself about all the changes I was going to make mentally and emotionally in my life, and I signed it. However, those were my personal goals. The problem was that I never asked God about it. I didn't pray and ask Him to help me. It was all about what I was going to do. That was a big mistake that slowed down my progress immeasurably. Had I prayed and gotten the Holy Spirit involved early on, I believe I would have made progress much faster.

Unfortunately, at the time, I just didn't know any better. But, thank God, I eventually came to my senses and finally came to the conclusion that I needed God's help. And even when I got Him involved, it still seemed to take an eternity for me to make progress. My emotional healing journey can be likened to priming one of those old water pumps where you had to pump the handle for a while before any water came out. After a while, by His grace, my emotions started to heal. As time went on, the healing came faster. I simply had to keep pressing on until I started seeing results.

I have come to the realization that in the process of becoming a whole person, it is normal to feel we will never get out of our mess. The devil perpetuates that lie so that we will simply give up. But we must be determined that by the stripes of Jesus, we will be made whole, and we are not going to just give up the fight. The key is that no matter how long it takes, we must make up our minds not to give up until we experience the miracle of healing and wholeness in our lives. You must be like Jacob and tell God you won't let go until you get your blessing (Genesis 32:26). Pursue God with all that is within you, and wholeness will simply be a by-product. Purpose in your heart that the devil will not keep you from getting what's yours as your birthright.

Another key to obtaining emotional healing is that we must continue to do whatever God has instructed us to do to facilitate our healing on a daily basis. It matters not whether it's physical or emotional healing, consistency is the key. Dr. Creflo Dollar says the enemy knows that he can defeat Christians is because many of us lack the ability to stay consistent. We can be faithful for a few days, but what if it takes months or years?[22] We must strive to be consistent until we receive our healing breakthrough.

For example, we have to be consistently vigilant over our speech. In the same breath it takes to say, "My leg hurts" or "I am so hurt by what so-and-so did," we can say, "I am healed." Are you speaking God's Word over your body and your emotions daily? We have to consistently live a healthy lifestyle spiritually, physically, and emotionally. Spiritually, are you "eating" on a regular basis? We all have got to spend time in God's Word daily. Are you reading scripturally packed literature and watching programs that feed your spirit? Physically speaking, are you eating right, exercising, and getting regular medical check-ups? On an emotional level, are you taking time out to reflect on the things that bother you, find out why they bother you, and refuse to ignore them or sweep them under the proverbial carpet in your soul? These are the questions that we need to ask ourselves because we need to be consistent in these areas.

We also need to be consistent in the area of our faith. Are you holding on to your faith in God that He can and will deliver, even though it's been a while and you haven't seen results? Just because wholeness has not completely manifested does not mean that God will not be faithful to do what He has said in His Word. Joseph was in prison several years before he became second in command in Egypt (Genesis 39-41). The Israelites had been in Egypt 430 years when they were delivered from the bondage of slavery (Exodus 12:40-41). The woman with the issue of blood suffered for twelve years before she received her healing (Matthew 9:20). Therefore, what makes us think that we won't have to wait for our breakthroughs in life? When what we want to happen doesn't happen overnight, we can't just throw in the towel and allow the enemy of our souls to cheat us out of our miracle.

That being said, we have to learn to be good "waiters." We must be willing to stand on the Word until we die or until the Rapture comes, if necessary. Everything but the Word of God can fail, and God said that His Word will not return to Him void (Isaiah 55:11). When it comes to the seed of the Word, we can be assured that it will not fail to produce a robust harvest if we will be diligent to do the part that God has given us. We must believe, speak the Word, and do whatever it is that God instructs us to do, and "through faith and patience [we will] inherit the promises" (Hebrews 6:12). As a result, emotional healing will be inevitable.

## REFLECTION

1. What, if anything, do you feel God is trying to tell you about yourself that you have not been open to hearing?

2. In what areas of your life do you need to become more consistent?

3. What adjustments in your schedule, if any, do you need to make so you can spend more quality time with God?

## PRAYER

Dear God, I thank You that You are the Lord Who heals me (Exodus 15:26). Please help me to confidently and bravely face what you desire to show me about me. Help me to resist the temptation of "busyness" under the guise of working in the Kingdom. I realize that I must spend quality time with You if I am ever to be changed into the person that You created me to be. Help me to be patient with myself. Help me refuse to give up until I victoriously experience the miracle of wholeness. Help me hold onto my faith no matter how long it takes, and give me the ability to consistently do the things that you require of me. In Jesus' name I pray, amen.

## WHY DID YOU HAVE TO GO AWAY?

*I loved you more than words can say.*
*Why did you have to go away?*
*I believe you're in a better place,*
*But I cannot seem to put a smile on my face.*
*I miss you, I miss you terribly,*
*To lose you was a horror for me.*
*With tears in my eyes it's hard to see*
*What's next in life, what's in store for me.*
*But I must go on, though I cannot bear*
*To be without your love and care.*
*I just have to take it day by day,*
*Why did you have to go away?*

"The righteous perish, and no one ponders
it in his heart; devout men are taken away,
and no one understands that the righteous
are taken away to be spared from evil.
Those who walk uprightly enter into peace;
they find rest as they lie in death."
Isaiah 57:1-2 (NIV)

When a loved one dies, it is such a painful experience. This is especially true if the death is sudden, if the person dies at a young age, or if they die without Christ. Even when our beloved dies after a long illness, we are still never fully prepared for that. In our grief, it is so hard to understand why tragedy has happened. We ask God for answers and when there is silence, we must be content to trust Him in His infinite wisdom. We must be OK with not being able to understand.

For example, when I went to Oral Roberts University, five people that I knew died within a five-month period. My mom's best friend died. Then my grandmother died. Then my godfather died. Then a beloved professor's wife died. Finally, the son of the secretary at the admissions office died. I was reeling. I did not understand. We prayed for the healing of these individuals. We held around-the-clock prayer vigils for some of them, and yet they still died.

One day I was feeling so down about it, that I started to question God and my faith. I decided to go to a gospel concert on campus that evening. While I was there, one choir sang a song that I had never heard, and have not heard since. The lyrics relayed that when we don't understand the things that transpire in our lives, we simply must trust God. The Lord spoke to me that day through that song, and at that moment I was set free and was able to move on.

Thus, our grief is sometimes exacerbated by confusion and unanswered questions that accompany the death of a loved one. In order for our souls to heal so we can move past our grief, we must receive the comfort of God and trust in His sovereignty. Healing cannot take place in a heart filled with reasoning about why a painful death event happened. There is no answer that will suffice. Furthermore, healing will elude a soul filled with mistrust in God's ability to manage the universe. Trust is an absolute necessity.

We must understand that God has a purpose and plan for every event that happens in our lives. He is loving, kind and good, and if he allows a loved one to leave this earth it's only for a good purpose. If the person that passed on is a believer, we are guaranteed it will all work together for their good and ours, too, even though it looks impossible in the now (Romans 8:28). A good example of this truth is cited in II Kings 22:19-20 (NIV) when Huldah the prophetess sent this word to Josiah, the king of Judah:

> Because your heart was responsive and you humbled yourself before the Lord when you heard what I have spoken against this place and its people ... [and] you tore your robes and wept in my presence, I have heard you, declares the LORD. Therefore, I will gather you to your fathers, and you will be buried in peace. Your eyes will not see all the disaster I am going to bring on this place.

Therefore, if a loved one dies, perhaps God has allowed it so that he or she will be spared having to live through an evil circumstance in the future. Of course, knowing this does not take away the emotional pain of losing our beloved. However, it may better enable us to accept their passing when we know that they are safe in the arms of God, and they will not suffer unnecessary hardship.

Whatever the case, we know that God specializes in making ugly, painful situations work to our advantage (Romans 8:28). Again, we simply must trust Him to be faithful to His Word and know that our saved loved ones are in good hands. When everything is said and done and the dust settles, we must have a firm belief in our hearts that we will still be standing, and everything will be alright.

## REFLECTION

1. Have you ever experienced a devastating situation that shook your faith and caused you to question God? What happened?

2. How did you resolve it in your mind and get to the place where you could move forward, and how did that experience enrich your walk with the Lord?

## PRAYER

Dear God, I don't always understand Your ways, but I purpose in my heart to trust You no matter what. Please help me to be comfortable when there are question marks in my mind. Help me be able to allow You to be God, the Omniscient One, and accept the limitations of my finite mind. I recognize that You are sovereign, and I need to let go of my need to "fill in the blanks" in my life. Let me rest in You, knowing that as long as You are at the helm of my journey, ignorance is truly bliss. In Jesus' name I pray, amen.

## CHAPTER SIX

# RELATIONSHIPS

The poems in this chapter deal with the most important relationships in our lives: family, friends and co-workers. Through these inspirational writings, I seek to make you think deeply about how you handle those relationships, encourage you to maintain them properly, and do what is necessary to enhance them. I am sure that you are well aware that good relationships are a priceless treasure, but just like the cars that we drive every day, they have to be well maintained if we are to go anywhere in life.

Lack of fellowship with the Father makes the ability to have true fellowship with others more difficult.

## ODE TO MY PARENTS

*Your love and support are precious to me,*
*You are my parents, you'll always be*
*Two special people, two meaningful lives,*
*You helped me to grow, you urged me to strive*
*To be the best that I could be,*
*You encouraged me to just be me.*
*I love you both beyond my words,*
*I'm glad I was given to you by the Lord.*
*Because of you, I'm here today,*
*I love you more than words can say.*

> "Honour thy father and thy mother:
> that thy days may be long upon the land
> which the LORD thy God giveth thee."
> **Exodus 20:12**

The Bible tells us to honor our father and mother. Many people have issues with their parents. Some have a difficult relationship with their mother. Others may have been abandoned by their fathers at an early age, and this has left them with a void in their lives. Whatever the circumstance may be, God said, in Exodus 20:12, "Honor thy father and thy mother." He didn't say honor only the good ones. Some may ask, "How can that be required of me after my parent treated me so badly? What was God thinking?"

Why would our God require that of us? He said in Matthew 25:40, whatever you do to one of the least in the Kingdom, it's as if you have done it to Him. Therefore, when we honor our fathers and mothers (even when they don't deserve it) because He said so, we honor God. Jesus also says that if we love Him we will keep His commandments. If we honor our parents, we show Him that we love Him. When we love and honor the Father, He will give us the added bonus of lengthening our lives here on earth according to Exodus 20:12.

Therefore, God is trying to get us in a position to be blessed. He wants to give us the land and then allow us to enjoy living in it. It's a question of what kind of quality of life do we want? Honoring our parents allows us to be able to expect to have a good quality of life. If we have bitterness and unforgiveness against our parents, that will end in sickness and disease in our bodies. We will be turned over to "the tormentors" (Matthew 18:21-35), and our lives will not turn out well. Our quality of life will be poor. Therefore, honoring our parents is a choice we make about what kind of future we want to have. The Word says God puts before us life and death, and He encourages us to choose life (Deuteronomy 30:19). That means we have to make the wise choice to honor our parents—even those who were less than perfect—if we want to experience all the blessings and favor God has for us.

The Lord is gracious enough to have given us His Holy Spirit to enable us to do something as outrageous as honor a parent who doesn't deserve it. When we make a quality decision to give honor where honor is not due, I believe that an anointing to heal us from the wounds that may have been inflicted on us by our parents is released. As we honor them, we release the Holy Spirit to give us revelation, insight, and the ability to forgive them for all of their shortcomings.

Some parents may be so toxic that, in order to protect that which God has deposited in us, we must love, honor, and pray for them from a distance. But as we honor them and "kill them with kindness," I believe that the anointing of the Holy Ghost also becomes available to heal our parents of their emotional wounds as we extend love and grace to them. The more we forgive them, the more freedom we will experience on an emotional and spiritual level, and the greater the likelihood that they will change.

So we know we are called to honor our parents, but what does honor look like? I have a friend whose mother physically abused her as a child. She had a lot of pent-up anger as a result. When my friend became an adult, with the help and healing of the Holy Spirit, she made the quality decision to forgive her mom. She began to just "kill her with kindness." She called her to check on her. She listened to her. She visited her and met her needs. Sometimes it was a challenge, because her mother still exhibited some of her old tendencies, but she continued to honor her. Eventually, the mother began to mellow, and finally she broke down and asked her daughter to forgive her for the way she treated her during her formative years. The only way that this was able to come about was because my friend chose to forgive and honor her mother anyway.

Regardless of how our earthly parents may have treated us, God is the best parent in the universe. I was sitting in church on Mother's Day a couple of years ago, and my bishop preached a Mother's Day sermon about God's parenting skills that has stayed with me until this day. He said that because you may have had a difficult relationship with your parent does not mean that you will lack in any way because of it. God will not leave you at a disadvantage because you did not get what you needed from your earthly parents.[23] Even the best of parents have failed in some way, and even if you had good parents, there is only so much that they can do for you. Thus, you can depend on God, the "Parenting Specialist," to make sure that you have exactly what you need to make up for what was lacking in the early years of your life.

In summary, the Word of God says, "When my father and my mother forsake me, then the LORD will take me up" (Psalm 27:10). Therefore, we can be encouraged that God will "re-parent" us in whatever ways our biological parents dropped the ball. With God's assistance, we can honor our parents in spite of their personal and spiritual shortcomings. As a result, we will be able to live a good, long, quality life in the land He has promised to give us.


## REFLECTION

1. If you have had issues with your parents in the past, have you forgiven them for not being all that you needed them to be? If you have forgiven them, how do you know that you have forgiven them?

2. If you have not forgiven your parents, why not talk to God about it, and ask the Holy Spirit to help you make the quality decision to forgive and honor them?

3. If your parents are living, what are some ways that you can you show honor to them?

4. If you have a difficult relationship with your parent(s), have you sought God in fasting and prayer and asked God what he wants you to do about that relationship? Have you asked Him to reveal to you ways in which you need to change? If so, what have you heard? If not, when do you plan to do so?

## PRAYER

Dear God, thank You for being my Father. You know all about the situation between me and my parent(s). I pray that You will heal me in the areas that I need to be healed as a result of what I did not receive as a child. Help me forgive my parents for anything they did to hurt me, knowing they did the best that they could based on how they were parented. Help me honor my mom/dad as You require in Your Word despite how I feel. Help me to allow You to love them through me, and I thank You in advance for the blessing that You have promised me in Your Word for my obedience. In Jesus' name, I pray, amen.

## A FRIEND INDEED

When God first placed you in my life,
The reason escaped me.
But as the time continued to pass,
I eventually came to see
How God blessed me with a friend in you,
You are a friend indeed.
The support and love that you've given
Have touched my life immeasurably,
You surely have helped me to grow in the Lord,
You've encouraged me to stay on my knees.
I'm a better person because I know you,
You are a friend indeed.
We are as iron sharpens iron,
We benefit mutually
From God's own infinite wisdom,
His blessings, His love, and His peace.
How grateful I am for His grace and love
That He lavishly extends to me
Through the gift of a dear friend like you;
You are a friend indeed.

> "A friend loveth at all times, and
> a brother is born for adversity."
> **Proverbs 17:17**

People. As the old saying goes, "You can't live with them, and you can't live with out them." God made us so that we need connection, but because of the fall of man, we all have a sinful nature and are prone to hurt each other frequently. How do we reconcile this dilemma? We all need friends and companions to be all that we can become in Christ. Friends sharpen us spiritually, help us to look at ourselves truthfully, give us a reality check when we need it, and promote our personal growth. That's what friends are for. God designed the order of the universe so that we would need each other, and there is no escaping that. After all, if we know Jesus, we are a part of the body of Christ, and our need for each other binds us together in unity of the Spirit.

When we are hurt by others, as we inevitably will be, we tend to isolate ourselves because we want to avoid pain at all costs. If we allow this to happen, we are playing right into the devil's hands. Satan would like nothing better than to divide us so he can easily conquer us. We have to fight against the tendency to put up emotional walls with everything that is within us, lest the devil get the victory and dilute the power that we have as a body of believers. We have to make a quality decision to work through the issues that arise and hold on to the friendships that we have. After all, they don't grow on trees. If we choose this path, hopefully our friendships will become deeper, richer, and more intimate as time goes by.

Dr. Henry Cloud, author of *Changes That Heal: How to Understand Your Past to Ensure a Healthier Future*, states that we should avoid the mistake of throwing away our friendships when they are less than perfect. He writes,

"If you have had trouble with going from friend to friend ... because you find some little flaw and make them all bad, work on staying in connection and working out the problem. Actively seek the good as well as the bad and love the whole person. Make reality your friend instead of your enemy."[24]

Therefore, friendships are to be maintained and cherished. My father used to say, "If you have one true friend in your lifetime, you are blessed." The people that God has placed in our lives as friends that encourage and nourish us should be considered divine connections and gifts from God. We should be grateful and make sure that we let God know that we appreciate them, and let them know how much we love them.

We should appreciate our friends because they are so necessary for our spiritual growth. I love having people around me who are strong in the Lord and never get tired of talking about Him. When we can talk about what He is doing in our lives and what revelation He has imparted to us in a given day—and have someone give us a spiritual perspective when we want to be carnal—that is so priceless. Friends like that add value to our lives, they are instrumental in our maturation as Christians, and God has made them an integral part of our ability to fulfill our individual destinies. We should not take those souls for granted, for not everyone can say that they have such jewels in their lives. Why not make it a point today to tell your friends how much they mean to you and how much you appreciate them?

## REFLECTION

1. Think of the friends who mean a lot to you. What qualities do you most appreciate in them?

2. Who do you need to call today and thank for the role they play in your life? Make that contact today, if possible.

3. If you have not told them how much they mean to you, what is holding you back?

## PRAYER

Lord, thank You for the friends that You have so lovingly placed in my life. Thank You for the divine connections that are yet to come. Help me never to take for granted those precious gifts I call my friends. Help me to be a good friend to others, to be able to adequately meet their needs, and accept them as they are. Show me how I can be a better friend. Thank You for being the best friend that I could ever ask for. In Jesus' name I pray, amen.

# SOME PEOPLE THAT YOU WORK WITH

Some people that you work with
Are just blessings to be around.
They make your day brighter and make you smile,
They chase away the frowns.
Some people that you work with
Will always have your back.
They're great team members who dare to care,
And compassion they never lack.
Some people that you work with
Will help when you're in need.
They minimize the drama,
They're professionals indeed.
Some people that you work with
You are really glad you met.
They will forever remain in your heart,
Those co-workers you never forget.

"Servants, obey in all things your masters according to the flesh; not with eyeservice, as menpleasers; but in singleness of heart, fearing God: And whatsoever ye do, do it heartily, as to the Lord, and not unto men."
Colossians 3:22-23

What if a survey was taken at your job? Would your co-workers say you are a blessing to be around? Do you help your co-workers when needed, or do you refuse to help them so that you can maintain a sense of professional superiority? Are you a source of drama in your place of employment? Or do you bring a calming presence? Do you conduct yourself in a professional manner and possess a spirit of excellence? Or do you just perform your job at the minimum level until it's time to go home, and then leave five minutes before your scheduled time to get off work? These are some of the questions that we need to ask ourselves if we are to be a good witness for Jesus Christ in the workplace.

Think about these questions: Do your try to make the most of your time at work? Or do you waste a lot of time surfing the Web and doing personal tasks that have nothing to do with your job? Do you do your best to conserve the resources at your workplace? Or do you—on a regular basis—take home pens, pencils, pads and rubber bands for your own personal use? Even though your employer may not be aware of your behavior, our God sees everything. He expects us to do our jobs as if we are working for Him (Colossians 3:23). If we steal from our employer by not giving our full eight hours, it's like we are stealing from God. When we take home office supplies, we are stealing from God. As Malachi 3:8 says, "Will a man rob God?" When we steal from our employer, know that God takes it personally.

Try this one on for size: Do you get along with your co-workers by applying the principles of God's Word to your relationships in the workplace? I remember the time, when I was a teacher at a local high school, that I privately confronted the principal about his excessive use of profanity in our staff meetings. He cursed me out and told me he did not care about my being a Christian. After that, I decided to apply the Word to the situation. The Word says we are to love, bless, pray for, and do good to those we call our enemies (Matthew 5:43-44). I went back to my empty classroom, prayed for the principal then and there, and asked God to cleanse me of any offense. The next morning, I greeted him with a smile as if nothing ever happened. I killed him with kindness in the weeks to come. I bought him a gift certificate to his favorite restaurant as a Christmas present. The cursing at the staff meetings stopped. By the end of the year, after I finished my contract, I told him I was not returning next year, and he said that he was sad that I was leaving. There is a lesson in that anecdote: The Word works. If anybody should be able to work harmoniously with others in the workplace it's the people of God, by the grace of God.

If you are a Christian, know that you are being watched by your co-workers continually. Don't allow yourself to be perceived as a "problem" in your department. Instead, be determined to make your workplace a better place to work. Don't stir up strife, or gossip about others. Pull your weight on your team, and don't complain constantly. Don't be a "stumbling block" for unbelievers. We are ambassadors for

Christ, so let's make sure that we are representing Him accurately on a daily basis while we are at work.

## REFLECTION

1. Have you ever had a conflict with a co-worker at your job? How did you handle the situation?

2. Looking back on the situation, was there anything that you would have done differently?

3. What Kingdom principles did you apply to the situation and what was the result? Cite scripture and verse if possible.

4. When you think about your workplace performance, in what area(s) do you need to step up your game with regard to having a spirit of excellence?

## PRAYER

Dear God, please help me to represent You well in my place of employment. Help me apply Kingdom principles to every situation and do my job as if I am working for You. Convict me when I get off track and allow the devil to use me to misrepresent You. I sincerely do not want to create a stumbling block for my unbelieving co-workers. Empower me by Your Spirit to be excellent in the workplace. In Jesus' name I pray, amen.

# CHAPTER SEVEN

## SALVATION

This chapter includes poems that highlight the resurrection of Jesus Christ and discuss how to become born again through belief in His death, burial and resurrection. If you know the Lord, this chapter will cause you to reflect on and appreciate what Christ has done for us. If you don't know Jesus Christ as Lord and Savior, I pray that by the end of the book, you will be inspired to make Him the Lord of your life.

God does not require us to be perfect, for we have Jesus as our advocate. However, He is adamant about our pursuit of excellence.

## JESUS DIED FOR YOU

Jesus died on Calvary
To pay for all of your sins,
He was laid in a tomb for three short days,
And then He rose up again.
If you simply confess Him as Savior and Lord,
Ask Him to come into your heart,
His Spirit will come to live inside you,
You'll be given a brand new start.
If you believe that He died for you
To pay for the wrong you've done,
If you believe in the Resurrection,
The righteousness of God's Son
Will be imputed to you as His own child,
Your spirit will come alive,
You then can walk in the newness of life,
And your soul will be revived.
But if you should die, you'll be with Him
In heaven, that's guaranteed.
Just give your heart to Jesus,
And you'll live eternally.

> **For God so loved the world, that he gave his only begotten Son, that whosoever believeth in him should not perish, but have everlasting life.**
> **John 3:16**

Jesus loves YOU. We sang the song, "Jesus Loves Me," over and over as little children. Do we really grasp that in the depths of our soul? Because He loved us, He died on a rugged cross to pay the penalty for our sins. The punishment that we should have received fell on Him. He suffered. Oh, how He suffered for you and for me.

When you think about how we were the guilty ones, but He got the death penalty, it just seems so unfair. That's like when you were little and one of your siblings broke something in the house after your mom told you all not to play, run, or throw things in the house. Did you go to your mother and say, "Mom, I'll take the spanking"? Of course not! In our minds, if they broke the vase, they should get the spanking, right? But Jesus took our spanking for us. That's what's so unfathomable. In Romans 5:7-8, the Word says, "For scarcely for a righteous man will one die: yet peradventure for a good man some would even dare to die. But God commendeth his love toward us, in that, while we were yet sinners, Christ died for us." As sinful as we were, He died for us anyway so that we could be redeemed, have fellowship with the Father, and have access to everything that He is.

Have you accepted Christ as your personal Savior? If not, why not do so today? You will have to give Him your life, but you get so much more in return. You will gain the King of this Universe as your friend and constant companion. You have unlimited and unhindered access to

Him. The best part is that you will gain eternal life and know that you will go to heaven to be with Him when you leave this earth. Jesus is calling to you. Will you answer?

If you are already saved and enjoying sweet fellowship with the Father, are you actively engaged in winning souls for the Kingdom? If not, what is holding you back? Jesus gave the Great Commission in Matthew 28:19-20. You know what God means to you and the benefits that you enjoy as a follower of Christ. Others need to know Jesus so they can find meaning and purpose in their lives and know the love of God that can heal and make them whole. Decide today that you will do what is necessary to come to a place in your walk where you will actively seek to win souls on a regular basis. God will be pleased, and you will be blessed in the process.

## REFLECTION

1. If you are not saved, write down the reasons why you have not given your life to Christ thus far.

2. Take this time to ask God to reveal Himself to you in a new way. Write down any thoughts that come to mind at this moment.

## PRAYER

Lord Jesus, I admit I am a sinner and I cannot save myself. I am asking You to forgive all of my sins. Please come into my heart right now. I believe You died on the cross to pay the penalty for all the wrong that I have done.

OASIS FOR MY SOUL

I believe You rose from the dead, and because I believe it, I am viewed as righteous by You. Please take control of my life. I confess right now that You are the Lord of my life and I will follow Your lead. Thank you for saving me. In Your name I pray, amen.

## REFLECTION

1. If you are saved, write down a brief testimony of how you came to Christ.

2. Looking back on your experience and the process that you went through in coming to Christ, what can you glean from that to help you win souls to Christ?

3. If you are not actively engaged in soul winning, what is holding you back?

## PRAYER

Lord Jesus, thank You for saving me. I desire to be obedient to the Great Commission. You told us to go out into the world and teach all nations to observe what You commanded us to do. Help me to keep Your charge in the forefront of my mind as I go about my day. Help me to speak a Word in season when You prompt me to do so. Help me slough off fear and my tendency to seek the approval of man so that I can move freely as Your Holy Spirit leads. Help me become an effective soul winner so that I can glorify You and help others to experience abundant life. In Your name I pray, amen.

154

## *HE GOT UP*

*He got up*
*When His battle in Gethsemane was won.*
*He got up*
*After saying to His Father, "Your will be done."*
*He got up*
*After being beaten down all through the night.*
*He got up*
*With the joy that was set before Him in His sight.*
*He got up*
*After being whipped and making not a sound.*
*He got up*
*'Cause the death angel could never hold Him down.*
*He got up*
*After lying in a grave for three short days.*
*He got up*
*Just to show us that He is the only Way.*
*He got up*
*With all power and all glory in His hands.*
*He got up*
*And He proved that He was more than just a man.*
*He got up*
*So we could exchange our sin for righteousness.*
*He got up*
*So that we could be imperfect and be blessed.*
*He got up*
*So that we could all be radically set free.*
*He got up*
*So that we could live our lives abundantly.*
*He got up*
*After giving up His life for me and you.*
*He got up*
*So we could get up and experience life anew.*

> **Therefore we are buried with him by baptism into death: that like as Christ was raised up from the dead by the glory of the Father, even so we also should walk in the newness of life.**
> **Romans 6:4**

Have you ever seen the commercial about the elderly lady who fell in her home and had no one to help her up? She yelled out, "I've fallen, and I can't get up!" That's a terrifying position to be in, isn't it? When we look at that woman's fallen state, we can compare it to the state we were in before we met Jesus. After Adam and Eve sinned, they were in a fallen state. That sin nature was passed on to us, and we too were born into a fallen state. We had "fallen and could not get up." We could not save ourselves, but because we believe that Jesus died on the cross and rose from the dead, through His sacrifice, we were able to "get up." In our fallen state, we were on our way to Hell, but Jesus took action and went to the cross to help us "get up" when we could not help ourselves. We could not keep the Law. We could not keep ourselves from sinning. Because of that fact, we were separated from God with no way of "getting up." Thank God for Jesus Christ!

When we were baptized after our salvation experience, that signified our identification with Christ. That showed the world we were unashamed to let everyone know that Jesus was now the Lord of our lives. When we went down in the water, it was as if we identified with being buried with Christ. When we came up out of the water, we identified with His resurrection. In Romans 6:4, Paul states that when we "got up" out of the water, it was time for us to walk "in newness of life." Jesus "got up so that we could get up" and show the world that it is possible to live a godly life in Christ.

I thank God for what He has done in my life! I was a broken, emotional mess for many years, but through His mercy and grace, Jesus brought me out to a spacious place. He's healed my body and my wounded soul. He has helped me to know who I am in Christ and has given me a revelation of my true worth and value in Him. I am sure that if you have met Jesus, you have a testimony to share with the world as well. It's our job to tell the world that He "got up."

Therefore, we should not even hesitate to give Him praise, Hallelujah! Jesus is alive! If you are a believer, He is alive inside of you. He wants to live His life through you. The same Spirit that raised Jesus from the dead now quickens your mortal body (Romans 8:11). Furthermore, according to Ephesians 4:1 (NIV), through the process of sanctification, you are enabled to "live a life worthy of the calling you have received." Thus, you can continuously experience new levels of peace, joy, and strength for living. When you get up every day, thank God that Jesus got up, know that your faith in that fact is the source of your righteousness, and receive the power to live the victorious Christian life.

## REFLECTION

1. In what ways has Jesus specifically helped you to "get up" in your life?

2. In what areas of your life do you still need help "getting up"?

3. Can you identify people in your life who need help to "get up"? Why not pray for them this moment? Think about how you will share Jesus with them the next time you see them.

## PRAYER

Dear Lord, thank You for dying on the cross for me. I appreciate the fact that through my belief in Your death, burial, and resurrection, I am saved and set free from sin. I thank You that You have made provision for me to be justified before You in spite of my inability to do everything right. Please let the realization of these truths sink in and enable me to walk in a manner that is pleasing to You. Help me to overcome every obstacle that Satan throws in my path, and help me to "get up" every day with a heart to serve and glorify You. May my life bring You glory and draw people into Your Kingdom through the power of Your Spirit. In Jesus' name I pray, amen.

# E P I L O G U E

I pray that you have been spiritually refreshed and hydrated after reading *Oasis for My Soul.* I have attempted to provide you with insight from my own personal walk with the Lord, and hopefully you have been able to glean something from the poems and inspirational writings that God imparted to me. As you go forward on your spiritual journey, I hope that what you have read will help when you are facing a trial or test. May God show Himself to you in unique and special ways in the coming days and grant you prosperity and success in all of your endeavors.

Our Lord is gracious, and He delights in the spiritual success and prosperity of His children. 3 John 2 states, "Beloved, I wish above all things that thou mayest prosper and be in health, even as thy soul prospereth." Prosperity and spiritual, emotional and physical wholeness go hand in hand, and I pray that you have advanced a little further on your journey into wholeness after reading this book. I want you to prosper in every area of your life, and I pray that reading the poems has helped your soul to prosper in some way. For when you prosper in your soul, the rest of your life will follow, including your relationships, family life, and work life.

If we prosper in life, we will enjoy our journey so much more. Those of us who have accepted Jesus as our Savior have embarked on a unique journey with the living God. He wants to help us improve in every area of our lives as we move forward on the path that He has given us to take.

I trust that the poetic and inspirational entries that have been presented will inspire you to be the best you can be for Christ wherever you are on your path. If you are going through a trial, I hope that you have been encouraged to hang in there one more day and refuse to give up the fight. I pray that you will be encouraged to carry on one day at a time until you see victory. If you are grieving, I pray that you have been comforted by what was presented in this work. No matter what you are going through, God loves you and He cares about you as an individual. You will surely come out on the other side of your test as pure gold (Job 23:10). God will see to it that you will be strengthened, established and settled according to I Peter 5:10. You have His Word on it.

Finally, if you do not know Jesus as your personal Savior, why not take time to ask Him into your heart right now? The ABCs of salvation are as follows:

- **Admit** you are a sinner and you can't save yourself. Ask God to forgive you of your sins, and ask Jesus Christ to come into your heart.
- **Believe** Christ died on the cross to pay the penalty for your sins, and believe He rose from the dead so that God will count you as righteous.
- **Confess** Him as Lord and allow Him to take over your life.

This will be the best decision that you will ever make. Once you surrender, you will have access to all the resources that the Almighty has to offer, and you will become a part of the family of God.

May God bless you and keep you in His care. May the peace of God be upon your life, and may you enter into the rest that Jesus promised in Matthew 11:28-29. He relays, "Come unto me, all ye that labour and are heavy laden, and

I will give you rest. Take my yoke upon you, and learn of me; for I am meek and lowly in heart: and ye shall find rest unto your souls." My prayer for you is that the wisdom that you have gained from this poetic journey will be instrumental in helping you to indeed enter into the rest of God, Who is *the* Oasis for our souls.

# When we lose our awareness of the presence of God, we lose our peace.

# NOTES

1. Joyce Meyer. *Enjoying Everyday Life*. TBN. WTPC, Virginia Beach, Virginia. Television.

2. "dehydration." By permission. From *Merriam-Webster's Collegiate® Dictionary, Eleventh Edition* ©2012 by Merriam-Webster, Incorporated (www.Merriam-Webster.com).

3. http://www.joycemeyer.org/articles/ea.aspx?article=im_ok_and_im_on_my_way.

4. "stronghold." By permission. From *Merriam-Webster's Collegiate® Dictionary, Eleventh Edition* ©2012 by Merriam-Webster, Incorporated (www.Merriam-Webster.com).

5. Henry Wright, *A More Excellent Way: A Teaching on the Spiritual Roots of Disease* (Thomaston, Georgia: Pleasant Valley Publications), 208-209.

6. Jentezen Franklin, *Fear Fighters* (Lake Mary, Florida: Charisma House, 2009), 26.

7. Deborah Smith Pegues. *Today with Marilyn and Sarah*. TBN. WTPC, Virginia Beach, Virginia. Television.

8. Joyce Meyer, *Do It! Afraid: Obeying God in the Face of Fear* (Tulsa, Oklahoma: Harrison House, 1996), 8.

9. Jerry Minchinton, *Maximum Self-Esteem: The Handbook for Reclaiming Your Self-Worth* (Vanzant, Missouri: Arnford House, 1993), 201.

10. Dr. Creflo A. Dollar, *Uprooting the Spirit of Fear* (Tulsa, Oklahoma: Harrison House, 1994), 80.

11. Myles Munroe, *Understanding Your Potential* (Shippensburg, Pennsylvania: Destiny Image Publishers, 1992), 6.

12. Creflo A. Dollar, Sermon. *Changing Your World.* TBN. WTPC, Virginia Beach, Virginia. Television.

13. http://thinkexist.com/quotes/maya_angelou/2.html.

14. Jerry Minchinton, *Maximum Self-Esteem: The Handbook for Reclaiming Your Self-Worth* (Vanzant, Missouri: Arnford House, 1993), 101.

15. B. Courtney McBath (2010). "What Do You Do When Your Rock is Not Enough?" Sermon presented at Calvary Revival Church, Norfolk, Virginia.

16. http://av1611.com/kjbp/kjv-dictionary/joy.html.

17. Granger E. Westberg, *Good Grief* (Minneapolis, Minnesota: Fortress Press, 2011), 13.

18. Ibid, 21-57.

19. William Backus and Marie Chapian, *Telling Your Self the Truth* (Minneapolis, Minnesota: Bethany House Publishers, 1980), 41-43.

20. "conviction." By permission. From *Merriam-Webster's Collegiate® Dictionary, Eleventh Edition* ©2012 by Merriam-Webster, Incorporated (www.Merriam-Webster.com).

21. "condemn." By permission. From *Merriam-Webster's Collegiate® Dictionary, Eleventh Edition ©2012* by Merriam-Webster, Incorporated (www.Merriam-Webster.com).

22. Creflo A. Dollar, Sermon. *Changing Your World.* TBN. WTPC, Virginia Beach, Virginia. Television.

23. McBath, B. (2010, May). Mother's Day Sermon presented at Calvary Revival Church, Norfolk, Virginia.

24. Dr. Henry Cloud, *Changes That Heal: How to Understand Your Past to Ensure a Healthier Future* (Grand Rapids, Michigan: Zondervan Publishing House, 1990), 202-203.

# INDEX

# ABOUT THE AUTHOR

Tracey L. Moore, M.A. (a.k.a. "The Purposeful Poet"™) was born in Newport News, Virginia and raised in Norfolk, Virginia. She received a Bachelor of Science degree in Industrial Engineering from Virginia Polytechnic Institute and State University and worked for several years as an engineer for a major electronics company in the Baltimore area. However, she felt unfulfilled in her engineering career. Therefore, she decided to pursue a career helping people through counseling according to biblical principles and obtained a Master of Arts degree in Christian Counseling from Oral Roberts University.

Tracey worked for several years in various social work arenas such as battered women's and homeless shelters, and also worked as a Housing Counselor. She also taught high school math for a brief time and continued to move forward in her determination to find her life's calling as the Holy Spirit would lead.

Undaunted and determined to self-actualize, she did much soul searching and decided to leave the teaching profession when God presented a divine opportunity for her to work for the Navy as a financial educator. This was a perfect fit because it harmoniously married her math, counseling and teaching backgrounds, and she was able to hone her craft for several years and become an Accredited Financial Counselor. After her tenure as a contractor for the Navy, she worked as a financial counselor at a major credit union until God orchestrated her departure so that she could pursue her dream of becoming a poet, author, and speaker. She currently resides in Norfolk, Virginia.

## Connect with Tracey

Website:
http://www.TraceyLMoore.com
Facebook:
http://www.facebook.com/TraceyLMoore2012
Twitter:
@traceylmoore1
YouTube:
https://www.youtube.com/channel/
UC-0A2_Ail4LICVkj3NHeAVA

\*\*\*\*\*\*\*\*\*\*\*\*\*\*\*\*\*\*\*\*\*\*\*\*\*\*\*\*\*\*\*\*\*\*\*\*\*\*\*\*\*\*\*\*\*\*

If this book has been a blessing to you, will you please
consider posting a review on Amazon.com and tell others
about what you have read?
Thanks so much!

# SCRIPTURE E-BOOKS FROM

# THE PURPOSEFUL POET

# (Please visit traceylmoore.com/store-2)

**DIVINE DELIVERANCE**
*Deliverance Scriptures to Fuel Your Faith*
**King James Version**
**(E-BOOK)**

Have you been in a difficult situation for a very long time? Have you been asking God for deliverance? This e-book is filled with deliverance scriptures to help you maintain your faith and believe God's power is on the way. An inspirational quote and a poem ("Divine Deliverance") by Tracey L. Moore are included. This is a great companion to the deliverance scriptures MP3 recording with the same title. As you listen to the scriptures and read along with the recording, you will be encouraged to hold on to your faith in the midst of your trials.

**GOD IS YOUR HEALER**
*The Promises of God for Those in Need of Healing*
**King James Version**
**(E-BOOK)**

Are you fighting an illness? God is still in the healing business! This e-book contains the healing promises of God for His children. Meditating on healing scriptures is like taking spiritual medicine, and God's Word pertaining to healing has been conveniently compiled in this e-book just for you. An inspirational quote and a poem ("God is Your Healer") by Tracey L. Moore are included. This is a great companion to the healing scriptures MP3 recording with the same title. As you listen to the healing scriptures and read and meditate on the Word of God, you will be encouraged to stand in faith and believe God for your healing.

**THE GIFT OF ENCOURAGEMENT**
*Scriptures of Encouragement for All Seasons*
**King James Version**
**(E-BOOK)**

We all need a little encouragement every now and then. This e-book contains scriptures that will encourage you in good and bad times. As you read and meditate on the Word, you will be encouraged to hang in there and fight the good fight of faith, and you will be able to use these same verses to encourage others. An inspirational quote and a poem ("The Gift of Encouragement") by Tracey L. Moore are included. This is a great companion to the encouragement scriptures MP3 recording with the same title. As you read and listen to the scriptures, your spirit will be encouraged. God's Word will help you gain the spiritual strength needed to continue to stand your ground on your own spiritual battlefield until you see victory.

**WALK BY FAITH, NOT BY SIGHT**
*Faith Scriptures for Difficult Times*
**King James Version**
**(E-BOOK)**

Romans 10:17 says, "Faith cometh by hearing, and hearing by the Word of God." This e-book is filled with faith scriptures that will help you to develop your faith "muscles" when you read and meditate on the verses over and over again. An inspirational quote and a poem ("Walk by Faith, Not by Sight") by Tracey L. Moore are included. This is a great companion to the faith scriptures MP3 recording with the same title. Read and listen to the Word of God on a regular basis, and you will be empowered by the Holy Spirit to believe God for the miraculous.

**PEACE, BE STILL!**
*Peace Scriptures to Soothe the Anxious Soul*
**King James Version**
**(E-BOOK)**

The Apostle Paul tells us in Philippians 4:6 to be anxious for nothing. Therefore, peace should be pursued by every believer, and this e-book contains scriptures that will help you maintain a peaceful spirit. An inspirational quote and a poem ("Peace") by Tracey L. Moore are included. This is a great companion to the peace scriptures MP3 recording with the same title. As you listen to the scriptures and read along with the recording, the Word you receive will help to cultivate the fruit of the Spirit of peace in your life.

# SCRIPTURE MP3 RECORDING

# FROM THE PURPOSEFUL POET

# (Please visit traceylmoore.com/store-2)

**DIVINE DELIVERANCE**
*Deliverance Scriptures to Fuel Your Faith*
**King James Version**
**(MP3 RECORDING, 7 minutes)**

Have you been in a difficult situation for a very long time? Have you been asking God for deliverance? This MP3 recording is filled with deliverance scriptures (read by Tracey L. Moore) that will help you maintain your faith and believe God's power is on the way. The recording includes the soothing, relaxing background nature sound of a babbling brook and can be coupled with the deliverance scriptures e-book (*Divine Deliverance*) for maximum spiritual impact. As you listen to the scriptures and read along with the recording, you will be encouraged to hold on to your faith in the midst of your trials.

## FREE BONUS GIFTS

You are a valued reader!
Please go to
http://www.traceylmoore.com/tlm/bonus_gifts.html
to download your free gifts!

Step 1: Please enter your name and email address.

Step 2: Click on the links to download your free gifts.

Gift 1:
A free MP3 download entitled "Please Heal My Soul." This includes a collection of 5 poetry readings by Tracey L. Moore (a.k.a. The Purposeful Poet™).

Gift 2:
A free download of personal affirmations with supporting scriptures to confess over your life daily. These affirmations are designed to help you renew your mind and develop a vision for your life.

MAY GOD BLESS AND PROSPER YOU!

Made in the USA
Columbia, SC
14 September 2024

41707862R00104